T A B L E   O F   C O N T E N T S

FOREWORD
Mark Searle

One of the risks habitually run by those who love the liturgy is that of becoming excessively preoccupied with the aesthetics of the rite. In extreme cases, some may even end up caricaturing themselves as musical dilettantes, choreographers or interior decorators. Of course, none are more quick to point out these excesses than those self-styled pragmatists for whom liturgy is a piece of spiritual business to be disposed of as perfunctorily as possible so that we can get on with what really matters, whether it be social action or parish fund-raising.

A book on fonts and how to design them may well arouse suspicions of fostering the expensive dreams of interior decorators, but Regina Kuehn has written a book that does far more than offer "ten tips on how to upgrade your baptistry." She draws on the riches of scripture, history and contemporary liturgy to unfold the *symbolic or sacramental dimensions of the baptismal font.*

Why is this important? It is important because, after about a thousand years of sacramental theology that put the focus increasingly upon certain indispensible words and the objects over which they were spoken, we have recently come to reappropriate a much older mentality which saw the whole rite *and* its participants *and* its timing *and* the spatial context of its unfolding as sacramental. Everything belongs to the sacrament; everything contributes to

the sign value of the rite, which is the medium through which God in Christ communicates with us. We do not merely receive sacraments. Assembled together, we *are* a sacrament; and the things we use, the times at which we meet, the places in which we celebrate, all come to share in the value of the sign.

Though the tendency to narrow the definition of sacrament until it encompassed only one minute, if indispensible, portion of the total experience can be traced back a thousand years and more, its full logic was slow to appear, for it ran in the face of the whole Catholic tradition. Thus it was only in this century that a combination of tight finances and diminished sacramental sense spawned the rash of shoddy, soulless buildings which all too often pass for Catholic churches. Even in the nineteenth century, where, for lack of imagination among other things, building a church meant imitating medieval buildings, there was still a sense that a parish community needed a building that spoke of more than itself, that directed the eye and the heart beyond the veil to the mysterious but vital realities grasped by faith. The building was a *sign*. Often enough it was, admittedly, a sign of ethnic pride, of Catholic chauvinism, or of simple affluence. But, for all its ambivalence, it was also a monument to the people's faith in the reality of the other world and, by that very

fact, a sacrament or outward sign of God's presence among and concern for the local population.

So it is with the baptistry and, at its heart, the font. This is no ordinary place, but the scene of our being made over in the likeness of Christ, of our being transfused with the same Spirit of God that hovered over the waters of creation and raised Jesus from the dead, of our being ourselves plunged into the mystery of death and of death's irreversible defeat. Whether we are baptized as infants or as adults, baptism makes us what we ultimately are: chosen vessels, components of that great sign set up among the nations which is the church. "Christians, remember your dignity," Pope St. Leo admonished his flock in the fifth century. The baptistry is an abiding reminder of what we once were, what we now are, and what we shall one day yet be.

A decent font is one that speaks silently of these mysteries. It is not a gimmick or an excuse for an indoor rock garden. It is, together with the altar, an abiding symbol of the sacramental life without which the church could not survive and without which the local church would not be a church. Font and altar bespeak the gift of life given us by Christ, and there is nothing more important, nothing more essential, nothing more to be valued than that. Font and altar represent the "source and summit of the

A PLACE FOR BAPTISM

REGINA KUEHN

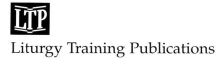

Liturgy Training Publications

Acknowledgments

Copyright © 1992, Archdiocese of Chicago.
All rights reserved. Liturgy Training Publications,
1800 North Hermitage Avenue, Chicago IL 60622-1101;
1-800-933-1800.

This book was edited by David Philippart, with assistance from Gabe Huck, Theresa
Pincich and Sarah Huck. It was designed by Mary Bowers, typeset by Mark Hollopeter
in Palatino and Univers, and printed by Associated Litho, Inc., Chicago, Illinois.

ISBN 0929650-00-X

Christian life," the most precious and intimate of all God's good gifts.

Though they belong together, it is a mistake to do as many churches do and set them side by side. While both are essential, they occupy different places in the Christian economy. The altar stands at the heart and center of the community's life and, ideally, at the center of its place for worship. Visibly it has to be the still point about which the people gather to become one. But the font traditionally stands apart from the assembly, sometimes near the entrance to the church, sometimes in a separate building, but always in a place apart, discreet, reserved. Today, as in the sixteenth-century Reformation, there is a tendency to insist that if baptism is important, it should be done in public view, but I am inclined to think this view to be false, both in its premise and in its consequences.

It is false in its premise, because it assumes that the most important things in life are conducted publicly, whereas the most important things in life—like birthing and dying, both akin to baptism—generally transpire in private, even though the fact of their occurring is often a matter of the most acute public interest and concern, and rightly so. Elements of the preparation of candidates for baptism have traditionally taken place in public because they involved the support and prayer of the whole assembly; and the immediate consequence of baptism, admission to the eucharistic community by the seal of the Spirit, likewise usually took place in the midst of the gathered assembly. But there is nothing in our tradition that suggests that it is right or proper or desirable that the mystery of birth should be attended by more than the necessary functionaries and a minimum of witnesses. In the classical Roman liturgy of baptism, the assembly, far from being passive spectators to the actions at the font, stormed heaven with litanies while the baptisms took place.

The consequences of believing that baptism should occur in the face of the whole congregation are also unfortunate. For one thing, it creates proscenium-style sanctuaries, where everything is enacted on-stage before a more or less passive audience and leads to a massive line-up of heavy symbols across the front of the church: font, paschal candle, lectern, altar, presider's chair, perhaps a second lectern for the cantor. It is essential, if we are to bring our ecclesial imaginations into line with the biblical ecclesiology of Vatican II, that we break that monopoly of symbols that reserves them all to an enclosed area "up front." Putting the font alongside or near the altar fosters clericalism, passive congregations, and a voyeuristic experience of the most personal of all the sacraments. The radical personalism of this sacrament finds its supreme expression in the nakedness of the candidates, where they are reduced to the human condition in order to be raised to the divine. In centuries when Christians were more prudish than they are today, it must have taken a much more profound realization of the meaning of baptism than most of us possess to make such nudity even thinkable. But the same profound realization of the meaning of baptism that led to ritual nakedness also prompted the creation of baptistries, shaped as mausoleums or as martyr-shrines, where the mysteries hidden from outsiders and cherished by insiders, could take place with fitting decency. These baptistries would be visited by the baptized on the day after their baptism and venerated on the anniversary of their baptism, but they were never intended to accommodate more than the necessary few.

Nonetheless, the most important feature of the font, wherever its location, must be its sacramentality. The blessing spoken over the font at the Easter Vigil is an acknowledgment that God "give[s] us grace through sacramental signs." As we have suggested, the sacramental signs of baptism cannot be reduced to the pouring of water with a form of words. Rather, the primary sign is the gathered church—the people actually participating in the rite according to their different functions—but what defines the church is the rite it performs and the place and time in which it performs it. The sacramental quality of the place, in particular, is not something that necessarily requires major financial investment; nor is it something that major outlay can guarantee to provide. The question is not whether we believe in baptism enough to want to spend a lot of money getting the right setting for it but whether we have a sense of symbolic realities and how they work. We have to know, and to expect, that the all too tangible and visible dimensions of the gathered crowd, the place and the ritual action fade before the reality of the intangible and invisible dimensions of those same things.

In short, a sacrament "works" when it speaks of more than itself. A baptistry "works," a font "works," when it pulls us up short and confronts us with the palpable reality of the world it represents and into which we are initiated by the rites performed there.

The great strength of Regina Kuehn's book is that it goes beyond aesthetics to sacramentality and re-introduces us to the symbolic language of the font as this developed in the scriptures and in Christian tradition. It is therefore to be recommended not only to those who are thinking of building or refurbishing a baptistry but also to all who wish to deepen their appreciation of the mystery of baptism and of the womb from which they were reborn to everlasting life.

INTRODUCTION
Regina Kuehn

Today we do not always live with strong religious images; consequently our parish life often is so uninspired and sad. Therefore, it is of great importance that a significant baptismal font make a permanent visual imprint on our memory. To create such a font, we turn to the artist who expresses visually the hidden reality of baptism. The artist (consultant, designer, architect, craftsperson) is called on to create a lasting image, a symbol that is strong both during and after the celebration of the sacrament, one that remains a constant prompter of our understanding of baptism. Such a font will not escape our mind and memory; our one-time baptismal *event* then will develop into a baptismal *way of life*.

The present-day trend of building "water theme-park" baptistries with abundant greenery and blooming plants—even silk flowers when real flowers are not affordable—intends to express the newness and freshness of life, but such arrangements often become merely pretty. They do not bear any sign of the numinous or carry the weight of sacramental character, nor do they allow us to sense the radical nature of our baptismal promises.

When building a baptistry and choosing a shape for a font, it is important to know that the font serves two functions. First, it *reveals* by its shape part of the truth about baptism. Second, the font *points* to the water. The water, in turn, reveals the mystery of baptism by its appearance, by the actions in which it is a part and by the words spoken to accompany the actions.

A Place for Baptism was written to be of help to all those who use a baptismal font or contribute to building one. That includes all Christians who make the sign of the cross on themselves with holy water when they enter the liturgical assembly and so declare their commitment to Jesus Christ and his church. The chapters of this book follow a pattern of liturgical instruction, including numerous photographs originally shown as slides to parish staffs, building or renovation committees, architects, artists, craftspeople, or even entire parish communities. Over several decades of consultation work in the building and renovating of churches, it became evident that the best fonts were built when all participating parties were similarly informed and singularly dedicated to making the font a strong focal point of the church's sacramental life. The approach of the book, therefore, is liturgical and pastoral, inviting design consultants, architects and artists to engage in, to understand and to prophetically express that life in its many dimensions. While many of the fonts pictured and discussed in these pages are historical, the chronological development of font design is not explored here.

If this book leads to confidence in making good decisions during the planning of a font, its aim will be fulfilled. Furthermore, those reading the text or merely looking at the illustrations will gain joy and spiritual enrichment at the same time. In this way, the book is useful to catechumenate directors, sponsors and neophytes who wish a deeper understanding of our rich baptismal symbolism. Finally, as more and more Christian churches are inspired by the signs of our common baptism, this book, like a pebble cast into the water, could help make ever-widening circles of ecumenical interest.

I owe a debt of gratitude to Gabe Huck, director of Liturgy Training Publications, who has suggested for years that my lectures and slides be published. Thanks are also due to Jim Wilde, former editor of *Catechumenate: A Journal of Christian Initiation,* who applied gentle pressure by persuading me to write the book chapter by chapter. Most of the chapters were first published as articles in the journal. Victoria Tufano, *Catechumenate*'s present editor, patiently continued Jim's pattern of encouragement. I am also grateful to editor David Philippart, who ensured that my Germanisms disappeared under the respectful use of his editor's pen.

A final acknowledgment goes to the many astute and imaginative priests, to the hard-working parish building committees, to the enterprising architects and artists, and to the many graduate students who asked informed questions and pursued the issues of font design with insights surpassing those that any of us had when we redis-covered the font a quarter of a century ago.

Throughout the book the phrase "place for baptism" refers to the font or its baptis-try. The font in its baptistry is a home for the church, a regular meeting place for believ-ers, a recognizable location to which one can point in memory of a liturgical event, a location from which energy emanates. It is a holy place that the assembly has claimed from an undefined area *(space)* and set aside for a special kind of first encounter. The font in its baptistry is like Mount Sinai, a place to which an individual is called for the sake of a whole people. It is the place where a personal covenant binds together an entire people and establishes once and for all the relationship of that people with God. When speaking about the covenant that God made with Moses, it is sufficient to name the place: Sinai. The very name of the place conjures up images of exodus and cove-nant. So it should be with the place where we celebrate our baptismal covenant. We call this place "the font," and in our parish any reference to this place should conjure up images of conversion and community.

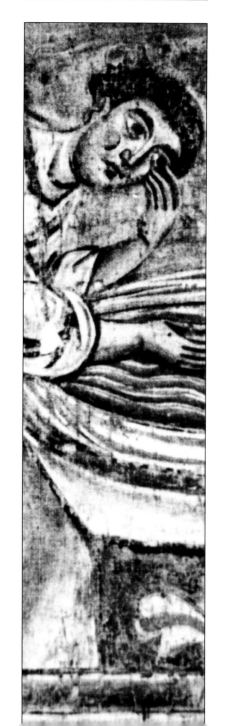

The Font As Womb

The word "womb" connotes a warm, cavernous, sheltering place where something can grow, develop to capacity and then be born into a new way of life. We speak of the "womb of time" where ideas are conceived and then develop. A mother's womb is the primordial place in which each offspring receives its initial imprint and pattern, influencing and, to some extent, determining its course for life.

Christians have long given some of their baptismal fonts the shape and the quality of a womb. In such fonts the mystery of faith is revealed by the very shape of the vessel containing the life-giving water. Perhaps it is the font's water, one with the life-sustaining waters of earth and the mothering waters of the womb, that makes the metaphor of the womb an appropriate way to understand the church's baptismal font, whether the external shape suggests it or not. Surely we glimpse here a powerful image of our tradition.

Mother Church

During the Easter Vigil, the great night of initiation, we hear the Easter Proclamation sung in the new light of the Easter candle. In splendid images the cantor sings:

> Rejoice, heavenly powers!
> Sing, choirs of angels!
> Exult, all creation around God's throne!
> Jesus Christ, our King, is risen! . . .
>
> Rejoice, O earth, in shining splendor,
> radiant in the brightness of your king!
> Christ has conquered!

The third stanza continues:

> Rejoice, O Mother Church! Exult in glory!
> The risen Savior shines upon you!
>
> Let this place resound with joy,
> echoing the mighty song of all
> God's people!

It is that same Mother Church who shortly after the Exsultet will call the elect to the water and give birth to many children.

The *Rite of Dedication of a Church*, 62, also praises the church as mother. Referring to the font, the prayer of dedication says:

> Here is reflected the mystery of the church.
> The church is fruitful,
> made holy by the blood of Christ:
> a bride made radiant with his glory,
> a virgin splendid in the wholeness
> of her faith,
> a mother blessed through the power
> of the Spirit.

1. Water—the primary symbol of baptism—is both life-giving and death-dealing.

1

2. Water fills out and takes the form of any container. When it is thus tamed, it offers peace and is a natural meeting place.

3. In ritual, water transforms and regenerates, as in the case of Jesus' healing the man born blind.

4

4. After placing mud in the man's eyes, Jesus instructed him to wash three times in the pool at the Temple — a ritual action.

Water: The Primary Symbol

Although this book focuses on the baptismal font, it must be said emphatically that the container is not the primary symbol of baptism. When we baptize by affusion, it is water that is poured over the person. When we baptize by immersion, the initiate is dipped (in Greek *baptizein*) three times into the cleansing water; and in submersion the candidates completely entrust themselves to the element of water to signify their dying to sin and rising into a new life with Christ. Without water there is no baptism.

This element plays a specific role: Unlike the "solid" part of our earth, water is alive and constantly changing. Its power can create and susain life, damage or destroy it. In the natural realm, its functions are manifold: Water cools and refreshes, cleans and invigorates, heals the body and buries living things. Standing at a river's edge we know that water is the medium for all that nourishes us, that it aids in transportation and communication, in accumulating wealth and power, and all the while shows its power in unexpected, often wicked, ways *(illustration 1).*

Water fills out and takes on any form that human beings offer to it. When we tame wild water for our need or pleasure, it offers peace and a natural place to gather *(illustration 2).*

When water is used ritually, it brings about transformation. It signals the end of an old way of existing, the beginning of life in a new community and the vision of life in eternity *(illustrations 3–4).* In an eighth century sacramentary named for Pope Gelasius (492–496 CE) the prayer of consecration of the font calls the Holy Spirit upon the water (much as we do

5. This large, womb-shaped font unmistakably is a place of rebirth.

6. This is the first font in Germany to have a scriptural passage in the vernacular etched into it—Ezekiel 36:25–28. Of poured bronze, this font is six feet tall.

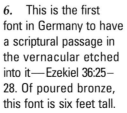

7

the womb-like water: "Take those who are to be born again and shape them after the pattern of your own divine beauty, the beauty no words can express. So filled with beauty, born anew, may they attain salvation and be considered worthy of a place in your kingdom." (Serapion, bishop of Thmuis, c. 350 CE)

Eastern religions and ancient mythologies also refer to the womb as a symbol of spiritual rebirth. Nicodemus knew something about rebirth. He meets Jesus secretly and asks the question: "How can one be born again in old age? Can a person return to the womb?" This question prompts the discourse on baptism in the third chapter of the gospel of John. This passage has had an important role in the development of baptismal theology. Christ solemnly assures that "no one can enter into God's kingdom without being begotten of water and Spirit." Translations differ here between *born* (or reborn) of water and Spirit, and *begotten* of water and Spirit. This ambiguity points to the depth of the images surrounding one's emergence into life anew.

over bread and wine): "Let your Holy Spirit . . . give fecundity to this water . . . so that, sanctification being conceived therein, there may come forth from the unspotted womb of the divine font a heavenly offspring, reborn unto a new creature."

Water in baptism signals the end of an old way of existing and the beginning of life in a new community whose vision is eternity. When we enter the church building on Sunday and consciously dip our hand into the baptismal water, we embrace this transformation again and again.

The Transforming Womb

The greatest agent of transformation is the womb; it changes the past into the future. Combining the two images, the water and the womb, a community makes a strong statement about the nature of baptism. An ancient prayer expresses this transforming work of

Womb-shaped Fonts and Immersion

Strong, simple images engage the viewer's imagination. A case in point is the font in *illustration 5*. It unmistakably says "cleansing is taking place here." Our memory complements what we see with scriptural verses such as "I wash you clean of all defilement," (Ezekiel 36:25) and our mind expects a large quantity of water to accomplish that.

The late Romanesque font of poured bronze in St. Maria im Kapitol Church, Cologne is six feet tall *(illustration 6)*. Ezekiel 36:25–28 is

8. This womb-shaped font clearly gives one birth into eternity.

10. This beautiful sandstone is, unfortunately, surrounded by carpeting.

9

9. Drains drilled into the surrounding floor make it easy to pour large amounts of water from this font over the bodies of adults standing next to it.

engraved on the lid. While today we know it is imperative for the water to be visible, other eras had a different approach. In the past, the precious water of baptism was safely guarded and its mystery veiled. The tight-fitting lid also served to keep the water clean in a time when water was less frequently blessed for baptism.

Illustration 7 shows a font with a sunken floor which can be flooded for the Easter Vigil. Baptism takes place exactly as in the carved scene of John baptizing Jesus by pouring a large amount of water over his entire body. The font in *illustration 8* invites the assembly into the awesome mystery of baptism. An adult speaking the baptismal vows at this font is perceived as entering into a covenant with Christ for eternity. If the wake of this person being baptized were also to take place at this font, the fulfillment of this covenant would be clearly imaged.

11

The font in *illustration 9* stands in the entryway of the church building. On Sundays the lid is removed. Markings in the natural stone suggest the action of the Spirit. The entire floor is stone—contrasting colors for death and life experience. Drainage holes are drilled into the periphery, allowing for the pouring of water over those being baptized.

The beautiful sandstone font in *illustrations 10–11* has ample room for immersion of an infant. Unfortunately, the font is surrounded by carpet, making no easy provision for adult baptism. The parish is considering various options: cutting out the carpet and providing drainage in a new tile floor, or moving the font into the narthex and incorporating it into a lower pool of the same design.

Because it is the place of baptism in a cathedral church, the womb-shaped font in *illustration 12* is flanked by a glass ambry large enough to provide holy oils to the parishes of the dioceses throughout the year. To adapt this beautiful font for adult immersion, it might have to be integrated into a lower pool.

The font-as-womb conjures up many images that parallel the catechumens' experience. The atmosphere surrounding natural childbirth describes exactly the mood and situation of the baptismal candidates: patience, high expectations, familial intimacy, a one-time event, privileged time leaving a mark forever, supreme effort, communal joy and welcoming, immediate need for care and nurturing. A fifth-century homily put this well in describing the adult being baptized: "As a babe from the midst of the womb the one newly baptized looks forth from the water. . . . This person is like a babe when lifted up from the midst of the water, and like a babe is embraced by everyone." (Narsai, Homily 21)

The fifth-century words inscribed on the baptistry walls at St. John Lateran in Rome sum up the implications of the font as womb of the church:

> The brood born here to live in heaven has life from water and the fructifying Spirit. Sinner, seek your cleansing in this stream that takes the old and gives a new person back. No barrier can divide where life unites: one faith, one fount, one Spirit make one people. A virgin still, the church gives birth to children conceived of God, delivered in this water. Washed in this bath the stains will float away that mark the guilt of Adam and your own. The stream that flows below sprang from the wounded Christ to wash the whole world clean and give it life. Children of the water, think no more of earth; heaven will give you joy; in heaven hope. Think not your sins too many or too great: birth in this stream is birth to holiness.

The poetry is fearless and exuberant. "Children of the water," we are called, and then told, "Birth in this stream is birth to holiness." The church knows well the language and the image of birth and knows it best beside the font.

12

12. To adapt this beautiful font for adult immersion, it may have to be integrated into a larger pool.

The Cruciform Font

Romano Guardini, the renowned German liturgist, recaptured in the early part of this century an ancient but long forgotten concept: The human body has an essential function in the liturgy. In his book, *Sacred Signs,* published in the 1920s, Guardini wrote in simple terms about basic symbolic actions, such as making the sign of the cross, taking holy water, kneeling in prayer and folding hands. It was his desire to preserve or to create for the liturgical assembly what he called *Symbolfähigkeit,* the ability to express oneself symbolically, to let appear on the outside what is being experienced on the inside.

In all his workshops, lectures and retreats, Guardini trained his listeners to think and act symbolically. This discipline enabled them to recognize not only that an outward sign, a gesture, was the expression of inner conviction but also that the sign, when repeated conscientiously, had the ability to sustain, for oneself and for others, the faith that it expressed.

Guardini's approach was born out of pastoral concern. In his era, an age of highly developed individualism, it was no longer considered "proper, useful or fashionable" to express one's personal or communal faith in "sensational and emotional ways" (that is, symbolic or ritual ways), as long as one personally kept in touch with God. Guardini feared that the parish—the place where faith was made real—would consequently become an impoverished collection of individuals instead of the embodiment of the living and acting Christ.

Sign-Making in Catholic Worship

Post–Vatican II documents express the same concern. The entire introductory chapter, "The Theology of Celebration," of *Music in Catholic Worship* (Bishops' Committee on the Liturgy, 1972, revised 1983) is devoted to sign-making in Catholic worship:

> We are celebrating when we involve ourselves meaningfully in the thoughts, words, songs and gestures of the worshiping community—when everything we do is wholehearted and authentic for us—when we mean the words and want to do what is done. (#3)

> People in love make signs of love, not only to express their love but also to deepen it. Love never expressed dies. Christians' love for Christ and for one another and Christians' faith in Christ and in one another must be expressed in the signs and symbols of celebration or they will die. (#4)

> To celebrate the liturgy means to do the action or perform the sign in such a way that the full meaning and impact shine forth in clear and compelling fashion. Since these signs are vehicles of communication and instruments of faith, they must be simple and comprehensible. Since they are directed to fellow human beings, they must be humanly attractive. They must be meaningful and appealing to the body of worshipers or they will fail to stir up faith and people will fail to worship the Father. (#7)

Environment and Art in Catholic Worship (Bishops' Committee on the Liturgy, 1978), likewise contains a directive for the arts and the body language of liturgy:

> Every word, gesture, movement, object, appointment must be real in the sense that it is our own. It must come from the deepest understanding of ourselves (not careless, phony, counterfeit, pretentious, exaggerated, etc.). Liturgy has suffered historically

from a kind of minimalism and an overriding concern for efficiency, partly because sacramental causality and efficacy have been emphasized at the expense of sacramental signification. As our symbols tended in practice to shrivel up and petrify, they became much more manageable and efficient. They still "caused," were still "efficacious" even though they had often ceased to signify in the richest, fullest sense. (#14)

Liturgical celebration, because of its public and corporate nature, and because it is an expression of the total person within a community, involves not only the use of a common language and ritual tradition but also the use of a common place, common furnishings, common art forms and symbols, common gestures, movements and postures. But when one examines the quality of these common elements, one finds that an uncommon sensitivity is demanded. For these common elements create a tremendous impact on the assembly visually, environmentally and bodily. (#55)

It is to this end—the recovery of symbolic expression in the liturgy—that the present chapter is directed.

Choosing a Cruciform Font

The decision to build a cruciform font is made not primarily because of the beauty of the shape. Architects often use the cross as a design element because of the well-balanced shape that appears when two lines intersect at 90 degree angles, but designers and planners of baptismal fonts do not choose it merely for the sake of harmony and balance. Rather, we select a cruciform font as a reminder of the cross of Christ and all its implications: the

suffering, the dying and the rising to a new life as it is presented in baptism.

Christians did not arbitrarily choose the cross as a sign of their identification: Both the fish (*ichthys*) and the lamb also were of primary significance. The cross represented the crucial event in the life of Jesus, the event that *expressed his character and the nature of his mission.*

In the Roman Empire the cross was an instrument of pain and degradation, of occupation forces and tyranny. For the Mediterranean peoples who had become subject nations, the cross aroused negative emotions. It seemed strange and unacceptable, therefore, that the Christian community would adopt the cross as its sign of identification. To those who had witnessed mass crucifixions, Saint Paul glorying in the cross of Jesus appeared inexplicable: "May I never boast of anything but the cross of our Lord Jesus Christ, by which the world has been crucified to me and I to the world. . . . I carry the marks of Jesus branded on my body" (Galatians 6:14, 17). The importance attached to the crucifixion by the early Christians became a subject of ridicule by their contemporaries. "Jews demand 'signs' and Greeks desire 'wisdom,' but we proclaim Christ crucified, a stumbling block to Jews and foolishness to Gentiles, but to those who are called, both Jews and Greeks, Christ the power of God and the wisdom of God" (1 Corinthians 1:22–24).

What made the cross acceptable to the Christian community, however, was the resurrection. The sign that they adopted was the empty cross, which pointed beyond the crucifixion to victory over death in the rising from the dead.

13. St. Peter with three deacons baptizing in a
cruciform font.

14

14. A contemporary cruciform font. The plants limit access to the lower pool.

The Christians turned a sign of defeat and death into a sign of triumph. Because these facts are well known, we often miss their significance.

In his *Mystagogical Catechesis*, Cyril of Jerusalem (315–386 CE) provides a parallel between baptism and the cross: "Having stripped yourselves, you were naked; by doing so, you also imitated Christ who was naked on the cross." (2.2) In *illustration 13*, Saint Peter is baptizing three candidates. Although damaged, the mural can still be seen to depict baptism by immersion in a cruciform font. The candidates are immersed in a large amount of water and are, presumably, naked. Three deacons witness the events. Saint Peter raises his right hand, as is done when attesting to a great truth, and two of the three candidates raise their hands in response, making their sacramental confession of faith.

15. Three steps lead into the water.

15

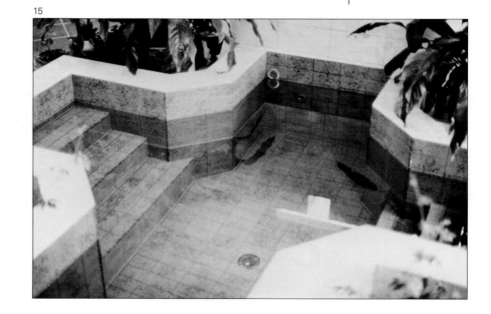

Clarity of Purpose

The mural in *illustration 13* provides a good model of a font that shows a clarity of purpose: to relate the baptism of Christians with the cross of Christ. Today, practical details in some font designs blur this clarity of purpose. The font at Saint Francis Catholic Church in Concord, California *(illustrations 14–15)*, was built within a spacious, light-filled, octagonal narthex that is large enough for a welcoming, witnessing assembly. The cross shape of the font is primary and is architecturally well executed. In the planning phase, however, the desire for a cruciform pool created a tension with the need for an easily reachable source of water for infant baptisms and for the signing with holy water.

In the resulting font, adult baptism is primary and normative, but two symbolic images compete for attention. The symbolism of dying and rising is seen in the cross shape of the pool—surrounded by the octagonal platform[1]—used for adult baptism. (This symbolism is further emphasized by the image of a rising Christ shedding his burial cloth—*illustration 16.)* The attached font for infant baptism symbolizes new life through running waters. These two images combined, in this author's opinion, reduce the strength of both images and blur the clarity of the cruciform font's purpose.

Adapting Ancient Models

In North America we have been building immersion fonts for such a short time. Many new

16. The attached upper font for infant baptism symbolizes new life through running water, but blunts the impact of the cruciform lower pool.

fonts—including the one just described—are courageous steps forward. Some recently constructed fonts, however, appear rather playful and fail to symbolize the sincerity and weight of the sacrament. In contrast, the font in *illustration 17* is remarkable for its stark simplicity and its placement in the midst of the faithful. The baptistry is located in the crypt of the huge Romanesque cathedral of Speyer, the resting place of German emperors. Simple cut stones are held together by metal clamps to create a large cruciform font *(illustration 18).* On the surrounding stone floor, water can be spilled and people can get wet. With this font, there is no impediment between the candidate and the sacrament, between the faithful and the font in their midst, between the awe-inspiring

event of baptism and the joy of being welcomed by this community.

Illustration 19, showing a sixth-century cruciform font in Palestine, provides a model that could be adapted for contemporary use. This font shows a clarity of purpose emphasized by the steps going down on one side and up again on the opposite side. The symbol is powerful and uncluttered; it needs no explanation for those who are steeped in scriptural images or in the catechesis of the church fathers. Saint Chrysostom said, "Baptism is a cross. What the cross was to Christ and what his burial was, that baptism is to us."

This ancient font enables the community to perform both adult and infant baptisms. Its above-ground, built-up walls offer sufficient

18

18. The four-lobed font is simply but beautifully constructed.

19. An artist's rendition of an ancient cruciform font. Three steps lead into and three steps lead out of the font.

20. The floor mosaic bespeaks paradise gained through baptism into the death of Christ on the cross.

20

security against accidents, and people need bend only slightly to touch the water when signing themselves with the cross.

A modern adaptation of either font could add a motor to provide a surface movement of the water, and a heater could be added in frigid climates. A conventional water hose could fill the font and then siphon the water out again for cleaning purposes, or more sophisticated plumbing could be installed.

Symbols and Stories

Some basic symbols, such as shaking a fist in anger or embracing when moved by love, require no explanation. Symbols that have to do with story will not reveal themselves fully until the story is known. The cruciform font in *illustration 20* is an example of this. Early Christians built the Church of the Memorial of Moses on Mount Nebo in Jordan to remember one of the greatest stories of the First Testament. On this rugged mountain ridge northeast of the Dead Sea, Moses heard the Lord say to him, "This is the land of which I swore to Abraham, to Isaac and to Jacob, saying 'I will give it to your descendants'; I have let you see it with your eyes, but you shall not cross over there" (Deuteronomy 34:1–6). Moses died on this mountain, and many healings have taken place there since.

Once the story is known, there is little need to explain the symbol of the cruciform font— this church's second one, built during its renovation in 597–598 CE. We see the connection between the death of Moses and the death of Jesus on the cross. Moses led the Israelites through the waters of the Red Sea to reveal the saving power of God, just as Jesus leads us

through the baptismal water to reveal to us his plan for our salvation. The Promised Land is symbolized by the fruitful trees and peaceful animals of the floor mosaic, an anticipation of what is in store for the baptized who are promised eternal life (For a discussion of the Memorial of Moses Church's original font, see page 41).

Without the story we would still have an impressive archaeological site, but it is the story that symbolically unfolds the covenant of our salvation and reaches us on a deep level. In the case of Mount Nebo, the scripture story opens up the symbol of the ancient cruciform font. Today the catechumens, gathered with the faithful Sunday after Sunday, hear the great stories of the Bible. In the rite of acceptance into the order of catechumens, the Bible is presented to the candidates so that they can explore on their own the ways in which God has always saved us and can build a way of life based on the scriptural vision. By hearing and reading, the catechumens are drawn into the saving life of Christ and slowly become one with him and with his mission *(illustration 21).*

Perhaps parishioners preparing to build a cruciform font should read the stories of how death and life are bound intimately together. The result might be a community that not only builds a water container with the outer shape of a cross but one that also builds a way of life on the scriptural vision:

> For if we have been united with Christ in death we shall certainly be united with Christ in a like resurrection. We know that our old self was crucified with Christ so that the body of sin might be destroyed, and we might no longer be enslaved to sin.

For whoever has died is freed from sin.
(Romans 6:5–7)

Paul clearly refers not only to a historical event, but also to a universal condition that is marked by sin, law, flesh, death and powers of the world.

When we plan to build a font today, we often worry too much about incidentals such as changing rooms, hair driers and mirrors. All our energy, our faith and our creative talent should be channeled into doing the essential: building a powerful font. And above all, we must sharpen our awareness for the symbolic language and imagery of our faith.

FOOTNOTES

[1] The octagon is another classic shape used for baptismal fonts. The number eight symbolizes the "eighth day"—the day of the resurrection. See chapter 5.

21. Baptism is a sharing in the cross of Christ that brings reconciliation.

The Tomb-shaped Font

There is no question that a tomb-shaped font is always relevant to the understanding of the sacrament. The power of the water, kept in a tomb-shaped font, is immediately understood and we sense the transcendence of the element. We know that we are not facing H_2O but a symbol of Christ's death and resurrection — and our own. One verse of the Exsultet, sung during the Easter-baptismal Vigil, points to the meaning of that water:

> This is the night
> when Jesus Christ broke the chains of death
> and rose triumphant from the grave.

This puts to rest the argument that a tomb for a font is a macabre dance-of-death image. Our tomb-shaped fonts should proclaim triumph over death *(illustration 22).* In scripture, tomb and resurrection always belong together; the suffering, dying, burial and rising are so tightly woven together that they are an integral part of the Christ-story: never part without the whole. On Trinity Sunday the church (neophytes included) hears a reading from Paul to the Romans (8:14–17) that "we are children of God, and if children, then heirs, heirs of God, and joint heirs with Christ—if,

22. A tomb-shaped font proclaims triumph over death.

in fact, we suffer with him so that we may also be glorified with him." *(See illustration 23.)*

In the *General Introduction* to Christian Initiation #6 we read of this relationship between passion and resurrection, between burial and rising from the dead:

> Baptism produces its effects by the power of the mystery of the Lord's passion and resurrection. Those who are baptized are united to Christ in a death like his (see Romans 6:4–5); buried with him in death, they are given life with him again, and with him they rise again (see Ephesians 2:5–6). For baptism recalls and makes present the paschal mystery itself, because in baptism we pass from death of sin into life. The celebration of baptism should therefore reflect the joy of the resurrection, especially when the celebration takes place during the Easter Vigil or on a Sunday.

The church has declared adult baptism as the norm. Therein lies the strength of the sacrament but also the difficulty for parishes who have so far experienced only infant baptisms. In these cases the image of font as tomb is hard to accept. Once it is understood, however, that infant baptism anticipates the total life span of

23. The baptized are heirs to Christ's resurrection.

the Christian and not only the washing away of original sin, the image of the font as tomb makes sense. In parishes with regular experience of adult baptisms, the scriptural texts on which the tomb symbol is based make the meaning of the symbol clear. They are being read and studied and prayed and learned by heart. An example is this passage from the letter to the Romans:

Do you not know that all of us who have been baptized into Christ Jesus were baptized into his death? Therefore we have been buried with him by baptism into death, so that, just as Christ was raised from the dead by the glory of the Father, we too might walk in newness of life. If we have died with Christ, we believe that we will also live with him. We know that Christ, being raised from the dead, will never die again; death no longer has dominion over him. The death he died was death to sin, once for all; but the life he lives, he lives for God. So you must also consider yourselves dead to sin and alive to God in Christ Jesus. (Romans 6:3–11)

That this dying to sin and being brought to life is a drowning in Christ's grace and favor can be gleaned from Paul's letter to the Ephesians:

But God, who is rich in mercy, out of the great love with which he loved us even when we were dead through our trespasses, made us alive together with Christ—by grace you have been saved—and raised us up with him and seated us with him in the heavenly places in Christ Jesus. For by grace you have been saved through faith, and this is not your own doing; it is the gift of God—not the result of works, so that no one may boast. For we are what God has made us, created in Christ Jesus for good works,

which God prepared beforehand to be our way of life. (Ephesians 2:4–10)

Likewise, the letter of Paul to the Colossians points to the triumph over the grave:

When you were buried with Christ in baptism, you were also raised with Christ through faith in the power of God, who raised Christ from the dead. And when you were dead in trespasses . . . God made you alive together with Christ, forgiving us all our trespasses, erasing the record that stood against us with its legal demands. God set this aside, nailing it to the cross. He disarmed the rulers and authorities and made a public example of them, triumphing over them. (Colossians 2:12–15)

And immediately Paul maps out the framework for the new life:

So if you have been raised up with Christ, seek the things that are above, where Christ is, seated at the right hand of God. Set your minds on things that are above, not on things that are on earth, for you have died, and your life is hidden with Christ in God. When Christ who is your life is revealed, then you will also be revealed in glory. (Colossians 3:1–4)

Paul continues:

Let the word of Christ dwell in you richly; teach and admonish one another in all wisdom. (Colossians 3:16)

This is exactly what the fathers of the church did in their catechetical writings, baptismal admonitions, and sermons: They instructed the faithful for whom they were responsible and planted in their hearts the mystery of Christ's dying, being buried, and rising from the grave, so as to anchor in faith their union with Christ and the hope for their own resurrection. The

24. A Roman sarcophagus made of limestone from the early third century.

25. This tomb-like font, built in 1970 of carnelian granite, is stunning. The baptistry is large enough to hold a wake.

25

ascetic Origen of Alexandria (c. 185–254 CE), St. Ambrose (340–397 CE), bishop of Jerusalem, as well as St. John Chrysostom (349–407 CE), bishop of Constantinople, and Theodore (c. 350–428/29 CE), bishop of Mopsuestia in Cilicia, describe the font as a grave, a tomb, a sepulcher. Chrysostom writes, "When we immerse our head in the water it is like immersing it in a tomb."

It is not surprising, then, to find the earliest Christian fonts in the shape of a tomb. The oldest font know to us, in the house-church of Dura-Europos in today's Syria, has a rectangular shape. This coffin-life font dates from the early part of the third century and reflects the imagery presented by Origen at the time.

If a building committee decides on a tomb-shaped font, questions of design and material are relatively simple to answer. *Illustration 24* is of a Roman sarcophagus (the Greek word describes a limestone coffin whose chemical makeup speeds up the disintegration of its contents). It is easy to determine the dimensions of a tomb-shaped font. Stone is always a beautiful material but often also expensive, unless the material can be taken from former side altars that become superfluous during a renovation. One of the most attractive aspects of a sarcophagus font is the fact that a parish can build it itself and reduce costs considerably. If a plumbing connection is preferred for easy drainage or to accomplish a movement of the water through motor action, it may be wise to call on an expert. The tomb-like font in *illustration 25* has such water-recycling equipment. It is stunningly simple; carnelian granite reflecting the slight ripples on the water's surface. Built in 1970, it was one of the first such fonts after Vatican II and has been an

inspiration for many others. Designed for a Benedictine monastic community so as to stand in a passageway between the lobby and the worship area, it allows monks to be waked there, with the coffin being placed alongside the font and the Easter candle at its head. This symbolism is so overwhelming that no attempt at explanation will ever have to be made.

A sepulcher-shaped font can also be poured of concrete or simply be built of wood, the inside lined with a heavy commercial plastic sheeting to contain the water. Such constructions, though sometimes temporary looking,

serve the baptismal action well, and are often more attractive than the most elaborate but small pedestal font or the temporary, punch-bowl version so frequently used at the present time. The latter will never reveal by its shape the rising from the grave as depicted in *illustration 26*, the final story of our salvation.

Building a tomb-like font above ground is preferable to a sunken font of that design. The former will always be visible to the congregation while the latter must be covered after use *(see illustrations 27–29)* to prevent accidents. Covering a sunken font rules out its regular

27

27. Catechumens await baptism in a sunken tomb-shaped font. A portion of the cover is visible.

28. Outdoor wells show that pool covers can be beautiful as well as functional.

29. An iron grill placed a few inches below the surface of the water would prevent accidents but still allow access.

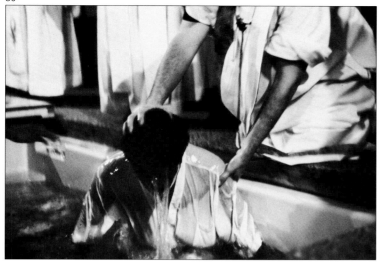

30. A tomb-shaped font makes it clear that by baptism we die and rise with Christ.

31. This above-ground double-basin font strongly alludes to the experience of rising from the tomb.

use by the people for the Sunday water rites. Granted, the Easter Vigil's baptismal liturgy is very convincing when celebrated around a sunken tomb font *(illustration 30)*. But the trade-off is too high for the rest of the church year because of the loss of a visible marker.

The above-ground double-basin font in *illustration 31* alludes strongly to the tomb experience. Located at the spot where the narrow entranceway opens up into the wide congregational seating area, it allows parishioners to dip their hands into the water, it invites infant baptism by immersion and it provides a tomb-like area for adults to have water poured over their entire bodies.

A similar treatment can be found in the double-basin brick font in *illustration 32.* Because the brick walls were built up high, there is not great danger of accidents, and full immersion can take place in the large tomb-like structure. The image of a sarcophagus is further enhanced by the dark carnelian granite lining of both upper and lower basin. Between the outer brick and the inner granite walls is a lead pan liner, installed to prevent leakage. The ambience of this font deserves notice. A wide area around the font is covered with brick flooring: It's acceptable to use large amounts of water baptizing here and no damage will be done by splashing. The font receives its light from a wide, floor-to-ceiling baptismal window. On the wall behind the Easter candle hangs the ambry, three-sided, to expose the three containers with holy oils. Large trees soften the starkness of the place, and a contemporary Holy Family group, accessible from all sides, attracts parishioners to walk into this area. An avant-garde stained glass wall throws constantly changing hues of colors into the baptistry *(illustration 33)*. This suburban church has a large membership of young families. Therefore the font is placed adjoining the altar area, though totally independent of it. The position allows the congregation to participate with ease when baptism is being celebrated during the Sunday liturgy.

32. While an adult would find it difficult to climb into this font, the brick floor allows for pouring a large amount of water over someone standing next to it.

33. The image of the tomb that this font evokes is enhanced by the carnelian granite lining both basins.

The Step - down Font

Planning an immersion font requires a courageous decision by a parish building committee. If the font is to be a step-down pool, even more courage is needed. The longtime minimal use of water has taken its toll on Catholics' ritual sensitivity. For too long we have expressed, for example, the mystery of dying and rising with Christ by touching the tip of a finger to a moist sponge on entering the church. Sunday after Sunday such small gestures have dulled our senses, leaving us incapable of experiencing the mysteries of faith in sacramental signs, and so we are fearful of them.

The fear of building a significant pool often is masked by objections of practicality: "It is not practical to use that much space just for water; the pool blocks the movement of the assembly; it is unsafe to use more water than absolutely necessary." How much water does one need to image God's saving deed of leading the Israelites through the Red Sea? To come down always on the minimalist side in decisions about the liturgy makes a silent statement that says, in effect, "We really don't want to get excited about God and the way divine life links up with ours. We would rather stay cool and detached and play down the signs of salvation instead of fully embracing them."

A second obstacle to building a baptismal pool is a great mistrust among Catholics of

34. John the Baptist baptizing Christ in the Jordan River. Angels look on from the right and river gods from below.

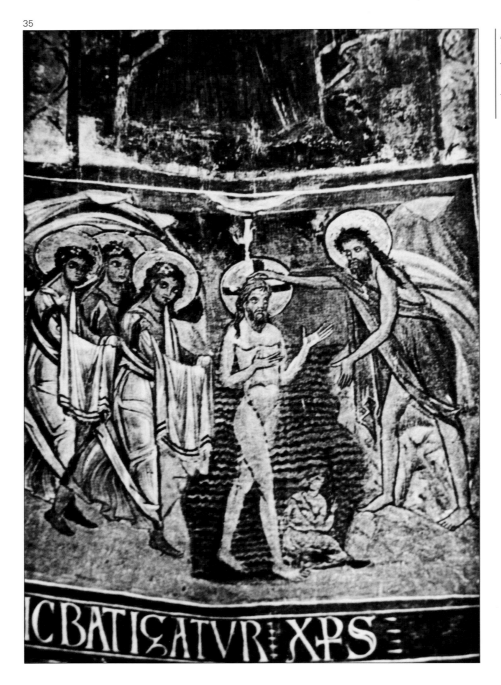

38 THE STEP-DOWN FONT

36. This unfinished icon shows Christ baptizing in the Jordan River. Scripture is ambiguous about whether Christ actually baptized—see John 3:22 and 4:2.

1982, they formulated the meaning of baptism in the Lima Document, using such terms as "participation in Christ's death and resurrection," "washing away of sin," "a new birth," "an enlightenment by Christ," "a reclothing in Christ," "a renewal by the Spirit," "the experience of salvation from the flood" and "a liberation into a new humanity in which barriers of division, whether of sex or race or social status, are transcended." This formulation expresses what all Christian churches hold in common regarding baptism and should lead to the elimination of fear and suspicion of each other, including the choice of a baptismal pool.

Early Images for Present Fonts

Another step in appreciating what all Christian churches hold in common regarding baptism is to become familiar with the practices and images of the early church. Looking at pools of the past, we are filled with hope for a strong future for baptism. Most of the icons, murals and mosaics from the earliest centuries up to the medieval period depicting the baptism of Christ show him standing naked in the water, often up to his shoulders. In *illustration 34*, the small figures at his feet are personifications of the River Jordan and the Dead Sea. St. John is baptizing from the rocky edge of the river, with angels in attendance who carry royal garments for the Messiah-King. The dove of the Holy Spirit is seen emptying a vial of oil over Jesus' head, making him the "Christos," the Anointed One, who begins his ministry at the prompting of the divine voice. *Illustration 35* is very similar. It is a mural from 1250–1270 CE. The parallels with our present baptismal

baptistries that look like Baptists' pools. Because Baptists choose their name from this central action of their faith, however, we would profit greatly by learning from their whole-hearted devotion to baptism and from their experience of descending into the pool. Refusing to build a pool in a Catholic church simply because it is a Baptist tradition reveals a deplorable degree of ignorance and suspicion in a matter of faith that should unite instead of separate the Christian traditions. When the World Council of Churches met in Peru in

understanding are affirming and encouraging: immersion, water and the Spirit, anointing, laying on of hands, the noble garment, a royal priesthood, call to ministry.

The unfinished icon of *illustration 36* shows Jesus himself baptizing from the ragged edge of the river, while those asking for baptism are up to their knees in water. He is touching their foreheads, imparting the Spirit, while his apostles act as witnesses. The lower part of the river shown here would make an impressive design for a baptismal pool. Such a pool would transmit the baptismal imagery of the scriptural stories and apply it ritually today. Several churches in Chile, including the contemporary National Basilica of Santiago-Maipú, have arranged for a rivulet to flow through the church building for the purpose of baptism. Such creative projects, referring back to the baptism of early Christians, make us aware of how trivial we have allowed many of our fonts to become, and how the sign-character, unable to enter into and influence our collective experience and memory, has suffered.

Ancient Fonts in Holy Places

On Mount Nebo, northeast of the Dead Sea, stands the church of the Memorial of Moses, a sanctuary that Christians built to remember the Deuteronomy events (Deuteronomy 32:49, 34:1). The new font in this church—built during a renovation in 597–598 CE—was discussed and pictured on pages 20–21. Here we will examine the church's original font, built in 531 CE.

In the original baptistry of the church, north of the ancient sanctuary, is a step-down cruciform pool surrounded by magnificent mosaics that depict floral scenes. *Illustration 37* shows that the pool is accessible by steps from three sides. The pool is three feet below floor level. One side of the cross arm holds an upper semicircular basin, probably used for the baptism of children. The pool is approached by way of a large carpet of mosaics—not pictured here—of hunters and peaceful scenes of trees, flowers and animals, possibly an artistic interpretation of the land promised to Moses. The most stunning mosaic symbols are found in the corners of the pool itself: four different interpretations of the covenant God makes with every person entering the water. They are intricate designs of inseparably intertwined lines and shapes forming a beautiful harmony: a vision of paradise, of eternal life intimately linked with God, of promises made and promises kept.

Two ancient pools also exist in Ephesus, in modern Turkey. St. Paul worked for almost three years among the Christian community of Ephesus that he established. Here in Ephesus he wrote the first letter to the Corinthians (cf. 1 Corinthians 15:32; 16:8), as well as the letter to the Galatians. Paul found in Ephesus some of the disciples of John the Baptist (who, according to a tradition going back to the second century, lived in Ephesus and was buried there after his execution by Herod). An altar was built over his tomb and many healings took place there. Subsequently, larger and more ornate churches bearing his name were built above his grave.

In the elaborate baptistry of the sixth-century church ruin of St. John the Baptist is an awe-inspiring pool in the shape of a cross (*illustration 38*). Three large steps lead down

38. This ancient step-down font is also cruciform.

39. Baptist churches usually have step-down fonts. Here, mosaic tiles are used.

into a cylindrical pool that is three feet deep, and three steps lead up again on the opposite side. The pronounced cross-shaped form is surrounded by three square openings in the floor, presumably the places where the baptizer and sponsor stood.

A similar pool can be found close by in the baptistry at the Church of St. Mary. According to early Christian tradition, Mary lived in Ephesus for the latter part of her life until her death (dormition) and assumption into heaven. Here two councils took place. This remarkable church was destroyed by war and earthquake and abandoned because silt had clogged the harbor of Ephesus, forcing the population to move westward. The church and the baptismal pool stand now in ruin, with prairie grass growing in the baptistry. Even so, the four-foot-deep cylindrical font, cruciform in shape with four steps going down into the pool on one side and four going up on the opposite side, still is recognizable as a profession of faith: By going down into the water, we are dying with Christ and are buried with him. By coming up out of the water, we ritually enact our belief that we now live in Christ.

The Baptist Church Tradition

Baptist churches are most familiar with step-down fonts. Baptist church fonts often have six steps leading into the water, six symbolizing the sixth day of the week, the day Christ died. The catechumen descends the steps (*illustration 39*) to stand hip-deep in the water and to address the congregation with a witness statement. *Illustrations 40 and 41* show the font, high above the heads of the congregation, ornamented like a balcony or ambo. After the

40. The exterior of this Baptist church font looks like a pulpit. Before being plunged into the water, the cate-chumen proclaims his or her faith in Christ to the gathered church.

41. The interior of the font is lined with tile.

42. A metal step-down pool from a Baptist church.

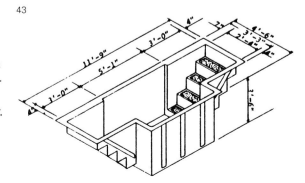

43

43. Step-down pools like those used in Baptist churches are available commercially. This model holds approximately 575 gallons of water.

witness statement, the catechumen is totally submerged (baptism by submersion) by the minister who accompanies the catechumen in and the neophyte out.

Many Baptist churches use ready-made metal structures to make a font *(illustrations 42–43).* These are often installed behind a glass wall in the front of the place for worship.

A Recent Pool of Significance

When ten churches on the southeast side of Chicago recently merged to form one new parish, deciding to construct a large pool created no problems. The majority of St. Benedict the African's parishioners had experienced the Baptist practice of using large amounts of water or at least had some familiarity with it. The decision to build a step-down pool was arrived at by a combination of fortuitous circumstances, pastoral vision and a creative spirit on the part of the architects.

The church building on the site had collapsed under the weight of snow, leaving the parish with an excavated basement three feet below street level. The building committee was determined to preserve the baptismal custom of submersion practiced in one of the ten merging churches. Taking these factors into consideration, the architects designed an unusual but very logical entry into the church: a spiral narthex, which requires that those who enter the building walk around the entire pool before they reach the worship area three feet below street level. The gently sloping ramp circling the stone embankment of the font allows everyone, including disabled persons, to enter with ease. At the bottom of the ramp, greeters stand next to the open waters,

44

44. View of the font upon entering. This magnificent pool is 24 feet in diameter and holds nearly 10,000 gallons of water.

45. At the bottom of the six broad steps, it is three and one-half feet deep.

46. A stone shelf at the entrance to the font holds the holy oils.

45

46

welcoming the worshipers. When the assembly is not present, a movable three-part gate of wrought iron closes the entrance to the water.

The round font is 24 feet in diameter, with the walls of the baptistry hugging it with a cylindrical retainer. At its deepest end, the water is three and one-half feet deep, sufficient to immerse an adult who is kneeling.

47

47. The font and the altar, in different rooms, are on the same axis. The altar is the ultimate destination of those who enter the font.

Eight wide semicircular flagstone steps *(illustrations 44–45)* lead into the pool. A circular skylight provides light.

As people begin their spiral procession around the pool, they sign themselves with the cross with holy water from the source: a large, hollowed-out stone partially pulled away from the wall of the pool. From here the water trickles down, moistening the stones in its path. Permanently displayed on protruding stones are a large shell, for baptizing infants, and the holy oils *(illustration 46);* the paschal candle stands at the pool entrance. The chairs in the worship area can be turned for everyone to witness a baptism in the adjoining baptistry *(illustration 47).* Moreover, the ramp offers room for about 60 people to stand looking over the wall for a full view of the ritual action. All sacramental celebrations are oriented toward baptism and begin at the font, including the funeral rites. A nearby table, adorned with carvings showing young and old people of the congregation greeting each other, holds a large "Book of Life." Here are entered the sacramental events, the names and the dates. Those who have witnessed them are invited to add their names to it.

Good Reasons for Building a Pool

As mentioned at the beginning of this chapter, the decision to build a baptismal pool takes courage. Such a decision demands a mature understanding of baptismal theology, one formed by images of apostolic times rather than by those of more recent Catholic baptismal experiences. From such an understanding, good reasons for building a pool emerge:

1) Walking down a few steps and coming up from the waters is a strong image of our dying and rising in Christ.

2) Stepping into a body of water links us to the baptism of Christ, who went down into the Jordan.

3) Responding to the readings during the rites, especially those of Noah and the flood or of the passage through the Red Sea, is made easier by the presence of a large body of water.

4) A large pool of water, a sign of salvation, cannot be overlooked; those who enter the church constantly must confront this sign.

5) A pool transcends the limits of being simply pretty and has the power to evoke the numinous.

6) A pool helps to bring baptism back into the consciousness of the people as a first-order, first-sign sacrament empowering us to live a Christian life.

7) A pool, because of its large circumference, allows more people to gather around and witness the rites celebrated there.

8) A pool could become the traditional place where sacramental, catechetical or spiritual events would be initiated.

9) A pool, because of its strong sign character, would be an ideal place for people to gather for ecumenical prayer.

Preparing the Parish

Once the committee has proposed a step-down pool, parishioners will need a careful introduction to the idea. For the majority of Catholic people, a pool is completely outside their experience. Only with difficulty can they visualize how such a font can contribute to the sacramental life of the parish and to their own Sunday practice. A reassuring pastor and building committee can do much to alleviate fears and help prevent ridicule. The Sunday bulletin, architect's sketches displayed in the vestibule, a special parish meeting and regular verbal information will transmit to the parishioners excitement and joy over the future font.

Beginning at the Beginning

Planning a step-down pool also requires that, beginning with the earliest sketches, the architect calculate the font as a below-grade entity affecting not only the plumbing, but the electricity, weight-bearing substructure and surrounding baptistry floors and walls as well. Only by considering all these factors will the pool turn out to be open, inviting and safe. Planning a baptismal pool cannot be an architectural afterthought. *Illustration 48* demonstrates that this is so not only during the planning phase but even during the construction period: While the scalloped outside walls of St. Benedict the African church were being poured, the pool and surrounding baptistry already were in place. This parish understands that it draws its life from the waters. It is serious about its building expressing that truth and forming parishioners to live it.

48. The font was built below grade. Before the walls of the church went up, the font was already dug.

49. View of the font from its threshold. This parish understands that its life begins at these waters.

49

The Octagonal Font

The word *octagon* comes from the Greek and denotes a shape that has eight sides and eight angles. In decorative art and in architecture, a distinction is made between a regular and an irregular octagon. Because of its ancient beauty, its concentrated strength and its energetic harmony, the regular or evensided octagon with 135° angles is the form most frequently used for baptismal fonts.

Overriding this aesthetic and psychological choice is a deep-seated perception of the number *8* as a symbol. Numerology, the study of the symbolic meaning of numbers, traces their influence on the human mind as they disclose a hidden truth without the use of words.

Most of the symbolic numbers that are used in liturgy and in Christian architecture are derived from scriptural images. The number *3*, in the shape of a triangle, depicts the Trinity: three persons in one God. Used in symbolic decor, especially on older fonts, it points to the threefold baptismal formula that invokes Father, Son and Holy Spirit, with the simultaneous pouring of water three times.

The number *4* evokes in the minds of Christians the four gospel writers. This number also recalls the image of the four corners of the world from Revelation 7:1. Four angels keep watch and hold at bay the four winds of the earth, while the faithful receive the sign of the cross on their foreheads. The symbol *4* conjures up notions of a cosmic event, as in the placement of four strong floor candles at the corners of the altar for the celebration of the eucharist. Without words the signal is given: "This place is holy; it brings together heaven and earth, angels and humans, the living and the dead, and signifies a great event of salvation."

The symbolism of *6* and *8* cannot be derived from scriptural passages but was developed by patristic writers, especially Ambrose and Augustine. Six is linked with the sixth day of the week, the great Friday, the day on which Christ died. Therefore, the design of many chalices is based on the hexagon, the six-sided shape. It symbolizes that this chalice is no ordinary cup but rather the cup of the new and everlasting covenant, which Christ validated on the sixth day by shedding his blood. (See chapter 6 about six-sided, cup-shaped fonts.)

If the number *6* represents the death of Christ on Friday, then the number *8* points to the eighth day, the day after the Sabbath, the day of resurrection.

Jewish tradition, by which early Christians lived, measured the week to image the creation story, beginning with Sunday, the first working day, and ending with the Sabbath, the seventh day, the day of rest. Christ's resurrection occurred on the day *after* the Sabbath and so did his appearances after the resurrection. This is why the early church gathered on Sunday, a working day, to remember these events in celebration and to await the time when the Lord would again appear in their midst.

This day's festive character was countercultural, a day beyond the known measure, beyond time, ushering in a new age. Augustine of Hippo (354–430 CE) wrote about this age in *The City of God* (Book 22, Chapter 30):

> And that seventh age will be our Sabbath,
> a day that knows no evening
> but is followed by the Day of the Lord,
> an everlasting eighth day,
> hallowed by the resurrection of Christ
> prefiguring the eternal rest,
> not only of the spirit, but of the body as well.

50

50. The power of this well-designed octagonal font is evident. Notice, too, the inlaid dragonfly in the upper left corner.

51. The chairs in this alcove can be re-arranged around the font when baptism is celebrated apart from Mass.

Then we shall have holiday,
and we shall see and we shall love,
and we shall love and we shall praise.
Behold, this is how it shall be
at the end without end.
For what else is our end
but to come to that reign?

Augustine characterizes this day still further: "This is the eighth day that surpasses description and cannot be foreseen, this day on which God will complete the work of creation."

Ambrose of Milan (339–397 CE), who baptized Augustine, noted that "not only is the font octagonal, but the baptistry as well, because on the eighth day, by rising, Christ loosens the bondage of death and receives the dead from their graves (*a tumulis suscipit exanimes*)."

51

The following octagonal fonts are presented as an invitation and encouragement. Simply imitating them would bypass the joy of creating. But seeing and understanding the different elements of their artistic composition will offer the freedom of experimenting with ideas and forms.

A Good Example in Context

The power of the octagonal font in *illustration 50* is evident. Stonecutters will notice that four slabs have simple 90° cuts and only four slabs needed mitered cuts, reducing both the difficulty and the price. To counteract the pressure exerted by the water, which pushes the slabs apart, clamps obviously and decoratively were inserted into the rim. The narrow, defining border on the floor level makes the difference between a heavy and a gracious design. Here the joints are mitered at the corners. This fine play of variation is the mark of good design, as are the modified cobblestones in octagonal pattern, pitted against the polished marble structure. Inserted into the floor here and there are stepping-stones with large artistic representations of insects. This welcome departure from depicting the life-giving qualities of water through the placement of greenery breaks open the spatial limits of the font. Insects normally fly or crawl around fresh water and what better insect to surround baptismal water than a dragonfly!

What fortifies this octagonal font is the cube from which the central water spout emanates. Placing basic architectural shapes together brings out their similarity and their difference: An octagon is constructed by cutting off the corners of a square. Finally, the water itself spews forth in generous streams, the sole reason for which the font was built!

Three Octagons

When baptism takes place outside of Mass, the baptismal place in *illustration 51* works in everyone's favor: The chairs can be arranged in the round for the readings and the signing with the cross can take place with ease.

Because the font is located in a large, open alcove near the altar area, the benefit of using it for the entrance and exit holy water rituals is largely lost. A chalice-type holy water font, however, stands at the entrance and immediately ushers everyone into the middle of the church from the wraparound narthex, thus forming a visual axis and sacramental connection with the baptismal font. Against the split-concrete block wall, the bronze font looks noble, well designed and skillfully executed. It is totally capable of bearing the weight of the mystery in the eyes of the people.

For more on how this font evolved from its initial concept to preliminary sketches and then its final design, see pages 92–95.

Old Materials, New Font

In a major renovation of the church, the font in *illustration 52* was designed to be built totally of marble from side altars and the old sanctuary floor. Marble does crack easily when removed from its original place. Therefore, special care had to be taken to glean enough material of the right colors to satisfy the design. The interplay of black and white creates a stunning effect.

In the creation of this font, which was positioned near the narthex doors, attention was given to the people's attachment to the old church building. The renovation plans led to the removal of quite a number of ornamental tiles, each depicting the symbol of the fish, to be newly imbedded around the two baptismal containers. They were originally located in the sanctuary floor, as was a large marble-inlay slab on which for many decades the presider stood for the celebration of the eucharist. *Illustration 53* shows how this marble inlay was cut down into an octagonal shape and made into the centerpiece at the bottom of the font. What an enrichment of the design and what a joy for the people to rediscover their treasure in a new and honored setting!

A view from the balcony allows one to observe the harmonious architectural interaction of the two octagons *(illustration 54)*. The choice of geometry was easy: It simply followed the many octagonal shapes already

52. This font was built from marble harvested from former side altars and the sanctuary during a renovation.

52

53

53. The beautiful marble inlay cross was once on the floor before the high altar. Now it graces the bottom of the font and all can see it.

54

54. The view from the balcony shows the integration of the two octagons.

55. Physical proximity to the altar is not necessary to show the relationship between baptism and eucharist.

present in the church, the prominent pillars, the wrought-iron pulpit, the light poles. The octagon then was confirmed in the new altar platform as well.

In order to achieve turbulent, air-filled water, several uneven ridges and grooves were chiseled into the overflow spout so that the water would not just glide out but would be agitated by friction at this point. As in many places, attention was given to the economical use of water, mostly for ecological reasons. There is no permanent connection to a water source or a drain. A hose fills the font and a hose with a self-starter siphon empties the font into the garden of the church. The only pieces of equipment are the motor that circulates the water, a water heater and a water pump.

On entering the church, one cannot help but perceive the strong connection between font and table, between the sacrament of entry and the sacrament of sustenance, between first commitment and loyal perseverance. The fact that this font is relatively far away from the altar yet still strongly connected to it shows that physical proximity to the table is not the only way to bring out this connection (*illustration 55*).

An example of an octagonal immersion font built from an old communion rail is shown in *illustration 56*. The two-level font is located near the main entrance of this cathedral church. Note the ample space around the font. This font is used for holy water when people enter. Chairs can be set up around the font for baptism celebrated apart from Mass. The beautiful marble portions of the former rail connect this new font to its building, and reveal a wise recycling of valuable material.

Three More Contemporary Examples

The octagonal font in *illustration 57* has some characteristics of a step-down font (see the previous chapter). The upper bowl and the spout are crafted of silver.

A place for the oils is built into the upper portion of the font in *illustration 58*. This upper bowl is used for holy water as the assembly enters the building and passes through the baptistry to the eucharistic hall. It is also large enough for the immersion of infants. The stained-glass mural behind the font completes the octagonal baptistry and depicts the story of salvation *(illustration 59)*. The baptistry is

57. This octagonal font has some characteristics of a step-down font. The upper bowl and spout are made of silver.

58. This bi-level font, located in its own baptistry, has benches lining three walls. Beyond the font is the back of the main body of the church.

59. A stained-glass wall depicts biblical water stories and the Holy Family. The holy oils are reposed on the upper basin.

60. A path made of broken, reconfigured floor tiles leads from the font into the main body of the church, showing that baptism leads to eucharist.

61. This new font was placed in the apse of the former sanctuary when the altar was moved into the midst of the assembly.

62. The upper bowl is generous—five feet in diameter and holding 50 gallons of water.

large enough to welcome there and bless with water the body of the Christian carried to the church for the funeral Mass *(illustration 60)*.

Placing the new font in *illustration 61* in the apse of the former sanctuary meant it had to be large enough to be seen from a distance. The upper bowl is generous for infant immersion *(illustration 62)*. But raising the large octagonal font on beautiful legs meant that adults could not easily climb in for immersion. A lower pool was added with a step for the minister of baptism. The catechumen kneels in shallow water and water from the upper bowl can be generously poured over the entire body. The minister can stand in the shallow water or on the step and stay dry *(illustration 63)*.

63. Since adults cannot easily climb into the upper bowl, they kneel in water in the lower bowl and have water poured over them.

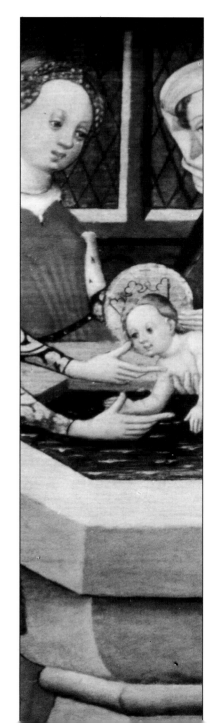

The Hexagonal Font

As noted in the last chapter, the symbolism of numbers is often invoked to remember and to visualize those things or persons or dates that are connected with particular numbers: the three persons of the Holy Trinity, the four evangelists, the Ten Commandments, the twelve apostles or the 50 days of Easter, to name a few.

Six-sided Fonts

Like other fonts discussed in this book, hexagonal or six-sided baptismal containers are created not only for their harmonious architectural shape but also, and especially, for their symbolic value. The six sides of the hexagonal font refer to the sixth day of the Jewish week. With the Sabbath being the last day, and Sunday the first, Friday was the sixth day. Early Christians kept this day holy by fast and abstinence and special prayers, for it was the day of trembling, the day when the Lord had won the world's salvation. He took on our burden and by his death released us from our sin, "the righteous for the unrighteous" (1 Peter 3:18), and thereby gave us hope for a new life. On Good Friday, Christ opened the streams of grace, empowering all the sacraments, especially baptism, which so closely images his dying and rising.

One Recent Example

Familiarity with scriptural and symbolic references lends clarity and a singularity of purpose to a planning committee. Such was the case with Holy Angels Parish in Chicago, which built the hexagonal font in *illustration 64*. A font carved from a single granite boulder,

64. This hexagonal font is carved of one piece of granite, left rough-hewn on the outside but highly polished on the inside.

64

65. A hexagonal font is built from the former communion rail, the panels of which have symbols of six of the sacraments, all except eucharist.

reminiscent of the simple fonts of antiquity, was selected. The hexagon, the symbol of the day of Christ's death, was chosen, not only because the church had been destroyed by fire and lay in ruins but also because the neighborhood, too, is marked by signs of death—gang violence, drug trade and racial oppression.

Against this hopelessness stands this perfect hexagonal piece of nature's beauty—and the faith community born from it. The opening of the font emerges from the hexagon in a circle, the architectural expression of perfection; the hexagon, symbol of the many Good Friday experiences the parishioners have to endure, is pitted against a symbol of peaceful resolve, of redemption and eternal harmony, the circle. While not every parishioner will be able to express such mystery in words, it may be perceived by all. This is the justification of symbol: It reaches beyond words and needs no interpreter.

Focusing even further on the death-life theme is the interplay between the rough, unfinished white marble floor and the dark green granite font, chiseled to give the appearance of an unpolished gem. The inside of the font is highly polished, which makes the container look wet and several degrees darker than the outer wall. The table surface (*mensa*) of the altar is made of the same dark green, rough-cut granite, making a strong connection between font and table.

Giving the font the appearance of a piece of sculpture is the "toe space" around the bottom. This appears to lift the tremendous weight of the stone off the ground and lends an elegant appearance to what could have been a bulky stone mass. A second beneficial effect of

this space is the access it provides. People can step close to the rim of the font—important when lowering an infant into the water or when extending a hand to the adult candidate entering the font.

The width of the rim would allow a parent to be seated there when immersing a child. Similarly, adult candidates could sit on the rim and bring their legs into the font without any difficulty, although stepping into the font with the helping hands of godparents supporting them is more graceful.

The font is positioned in the middle aisle at the entrance of the church, under a lowered roof. That position grants the font its own place and allows chairs from the adjoining nave to be arranged around it for the rite of baptism when it takes place outside Mass or for other gatherings.

No attempt has been made to connect the font to a water source. Filling and emptying is accomplished with the help of a water hose with a small syphon. The water is drained into a courtyard garden. This parish chose not to include a permanent water source for two reasons: The solid stone, unlike some other materials, is permanently leakproof; and the high price of a plumbing installation was avoided. The movement of the water, which might otherwise be accomplished by a motor, occurs when the parishioners dip their hands into the water, which they do in great number.

New Treasures from Old

Reasons for selecting a hexagon font vary. *Illustration 65* shows another font in the process of being built. The logic for choosing this six-sided font was simply the fact that six

66. This medieval tapestry shows infant baptism by immersion into a hexagonal font.

panels of precious Botticino marble were still in place as the communion rail of the chapel of a motherhouse church in Wheaton, Illinois. Every time the subject of removing the rail came up, it was rejected. The community treasured the communion rail because each panel was inlaid with a symbol of one of the sacraments except for the eucharist, which was symbolized in the altar. Shifting their treasure from altar rail to font was acceptable to the community after the members became committed to building a powerful font. Symbols of the sacraments are not foreign to a place of baptism, since the first sacrament opens up the access to the others.

The photograph shows the six panels being set up according to the design marked on the floor, which has already been covered by a waterproof rubber liner, reinforced by fiber and bonded by tar. During the building process, great care was taken not to damage the rubber liner, which would have created leakage problems. For the complete story of how this font was eventually constructed, see chapter 8.

Preserving a church's treasures and reusing them in a different context usually will gain the approval of the parish. The question of artistic quality often is harder to answer. Considering that a community usually builds a font but once, the criteria for appropriateness should be set high.

Refashioning a Pedestal Font

Most American adults were baptized as children in hexagonal pedestal fonts similar to the one in *illustration 66*, which shows a detail of a

67

67. A bishop baptizes St. Ursula by immersion into a hexagonal font.

tapestry in the Metropolitan Museum of Art. In a beautiful gesture, the priest dips or dunks (*baptizein* in Greek) the infant face down, while the parents celebrate the fruit of their marriage by holding hands. This is one of the finest images of infant baptism in this country.

An oil painting from 1450 CE, depicting the baptism of St. Ursula, shows that hexagonal fonts can be of a large enough scale for infant baptism *(illustration 67)*. The baptism of Ursula's companions—depicted in *illustration 68*—shows adults being baptized by immersion in a hexagonal font. Most contemporary hexagonal pedestal fonts are not of this scale, though.

Even though many pedestal fonts were created with great care and artistic talent, such fonts have become insufficient. Some of them have been refashioned without much effort by surrounding them with a pool of water as shown in *illustration 69* or, better still, by lifting the bowl off the pedestal and removing the font cover. Then the bowl is placed on the rim of a lower pool, built large enough for adult immersion *(illustration 70)*. One or several spouts may be drilled into the upper bowl to allow the water to circulate. The lower pool, built new, can be adapted to the style of the original bowl so that the new font harmonizes

68

68. The companions of St. Ursula are baptized together by immersion in a hexagonal font.

69

69. Fonts too small for adult immersion can be mounted inside larger pools.

70

70. The original font in this church—too small for immersion—is now the upper portion of a large octagonal font.

with the old. Such a two-level arrangement allows the baptizer to baptize without entering the water, and the assembly to sign themselves with holy water from the upper font. Parishioners usually receive the refashioning of their baptismal bowl with gratitude for the respect shown to the tradition of the many families whose children were baptized there and with excitement for the generous use of water that makes it possible to grow in the grace and the understanding of the sacrament.

An Affordable Option

If a community desires an immersion font but there is no precious building material to be gleaned from the church and the budget is low, another route can be taken: *Illustration 71* shows a number of large hexagonal containers. They are commercially produced, made of aggregate stone and very affordable. One such container, placed on a cube that might be covered with decorative tiles, would make a fine font of appropriate size and height. The arrangement shown, on the plaza of the Emperors' Memorial Church in Berlin, is made more attractive by the surrounding pavement, an irregular mixture of different sized stepping stones and cobblestones. It is as attractive as the font inside this landmark church.

71

71. Made of aggregate stone and commercially sold, these hexagonal containers provide a low-cost option for an immersion font.

The Font As Tub

The baptism of Christians is rooted in the New Testament. But the texts do not offer much description of the rite. It is presumed that Jesus was baptized in that part of the Jordan River which is shallow and marshy. Early Christian baptism, unless it took place in pools and rivers, was conducted in house churches, those of Roman origin being equipped with a shallow pool fed by rainwater similar to the house church of Dura-Europos, which contains the ruins of the first known baptismal pool (ca. 250 CE). Like the River Jordan, these were rather shallow bodies of water. Later baptistries, by contrast, as the one at St. John Lateran (ca. 500 CE) were not only significant in their imagery (steps leading down into the pool and out again on the opposite side, to signify dying and rising) but also by the large amount of water they held.

Contemplating the Greek verb *baptizein* allows a variety of interpretations concerning the amount of water required to meet and serve its meaning, whether it is rendered immerse, bathe, wash or drown.

Even if the New Testament does not yield any direct information on any of the details which interest us today when building and using a font, the *Didaché* does. This document, traditionally dated anywhere from 70 CE to the beginning of the second century, is a "church order" that offers guidelines. Its directions for baptisms are flexible and logical. "Baptize in running water," the *Didaché* says. "If you do not have any running water, baptize in some other. If you cannot baptize in cold water, then use warm water. If you have neither, then pour water over the body three times." (7, 1–3) Running, cold water is preferred for the sensual shock it provides.

Contemporary instructions on how to build and consequently use a font, are spelled out clearly in #76 and #77 of *Environment and Art in Catholic Worship*, promulgated in 1978 by the National Conference of Catholic Bishops. The guidelines have a great urgency that stems from concern over the decline of the sign character of this first sacrament. Such a decline is readily seen in the reduced size of fonts and the minimal use of water. The document shows a strong desire to restore the signification of the sacrament to its original vigor:

> To speak of symbols and of sacramental signification is to indicate that immersion is the fuller and more appropriate symbolic action in baptism. New baptismal fonts, therefore, should be constructed to allow for the pouring of water over the entire body of a child or adult. Where fonts are not so constructed, the use of a portable one is recommended.
>
> The place of the font, whether it is an area near the main entrance of the liturgical space or one in the midst of the congregation, should facilitate full congregational participation, regularly in the Easter Vigil. If the baptismal space is in a gathering place or entrance way it can have living, moving water, and include provision for warming the water for immersion. When a portable font is used, it should be placed for maximum visibility and audibility, without crowding or obscuring the altar, ambo and chair. (#76–77)

The key sentence for font builders in these two paragraphs of *Environment and Art in Catholic Worship* seems to be that "a font should be so constructed to allow for the pouring of water over the entire body of a child or adult." This makes physically possible a ritual bathing, a washing away of sins. Our Creed gives only one sentence to identify the effect of baptism: "We believe in one baptism for the forgiveness of sins." While forgiveness of sins is an element in all sacraments, it is primary in baptism as the beginning of our life in Christ. To be like him, free of sin, is a principal requirement to participate in his mission. Jesus' own baptism by John was the inaugural act of his mission and his identification with the sinful.

The water container where such washing can take place is most naturally a tub-like vessel. Each civilization has its own way to wash and bathe and to make, beyond the given objective of becoming clean, the connection with basic images of ritual cleansing. Our present culture, which favors bathtubs and hot tubs built of a great variety of materials, certainly makes it easy for us to understand ritual cleansing in a tub-like vessel.

To justify the choice of a tub font, look to the rich imagery of the manifold effects of baptism. Thinking of infant baptism first would be a limiting approach, since adult baptism is the norm. The introduction to the *Rite of Christian Initiation of Adults* (RCIA), therefore, offers a concise outline of the context: Chapters 1, 2 and 5 formulate the effects of baptism. For many building committee members, reading these texts together could be a unique occasion to talk about the first sacrament and its awesome effects.

Baptism, "the cleansing with water by the power of the living word," washes away every stain of sin, original and personal, according to Paul's letter to the Ephesians:

"Christ loved the church and gave himself up for her, in order to make her holy by cleansing her with the washing of water by the word so as to present the church to himself in splendor, without a spot or wrinkle or anything of that sort." (5:26)

Such a sentence dispels the accusations of some church members who, when faced with the concept of a sacred font in which sins are washed away, accuse the church of a morbid clinging to thoughts of sinfulness instead of a joyful celebration of new life. The Exsultet proclaims how such new life is not ours except in the forgiveness of sins: "O happy fault, O necessary sin of Adam which gained for us so great a redeemer!" sings the church during the baptismal feast par excellence. As the baptismal candidates wait to enter the cleansing waters, the church continues, saying: "The power of this holy night dispels all evil, washes guilt away, restores lost innocence, brings mourners joy; it casts out hatred, brings us peace, and humbles earthly pride." Hardly the language of a morbid church! During that night the church totally identifies herself with the poetic vision of Ezekiel (36:16–28) in one of the most beautiful passages of scripture: "I will pour clear water over you, I will wash you clean of your defilement. A new heart I will give to you. I will place a new spirit within you, taking from your bodies your stony hearts. You shall be my people, and I will be your God."

The intercessions for the candidates place, in a more prosaic language, the same imploring thought before God during the prayers of the people: "Through baptism, wash away their sins and make them holy." (RCIA, 380) And the conclusion to this, spoken by the presider, again implores God: "Forgive all their sins, adopt them as your own and count them among your holy people." (RCIA, 381)

Reflecting on such texts is a cornerstone of good planning and should never be considered as a waste of time in preparation or building a font, and building, in the process, a community not only agreeing to but enthuastically accepting a proposed design.

The following will examine some tub-shaped fonts and probe how well they support the image of being washed clean.

A Pre–Vatican II Example

Even today we consider the font from Switzerland in *illustration 72*, built in the early years of liturgical renewal, a precious gift. The simple tub is slightly elevated by ornamental feet. A former bronze lid has now been permanently removed to make the water visible and to strengthen the image of being washed clean.

This is a big font with an inner diameter of five feet (and it was built at a time when fonts were designed just big enough to sprinkle an infant). Big fonts allow big thoughts and big expectations. "Though your sins are scarlet," (Isaiah 1:18) they can be washed away here. Its sandstone was quarried from a mountain range near the church, a very attractive approach, giving prominence to local materials and honor to the local workers who unearthed it. Masterfully chiseled into the outer surface are two principal elements effecting the cleaning in this font: symbols of water and word. Each Christian era has its own great fonts. This one, in a genuine simplicity that omits all unessentials, is a jewel from a time long before Vatican II began to formulate the principles for immersion fonts. It still inspires us today.

72

72. This simple tub sits on four ornamental feet.

Contemporary Tub Fonts

Illustration 73 shows the first large tub font built in the archdiocese of Chicago. It is located close to the side entrance, placing two of the sacraments of initiation, font and table, into one line of view. The majority of the people enter there from a large parking lot, walking first through a generous lobby. Placing a hand into the water is the usual gesture upon entry. Altar, ambo and font are all crafted of black granite. The design of the font is one of the simplest and most effective: In spite of its diameter of over five feet it does not look heavy because the tub is elevated on four substantial feet cut out of the same block, allowing for toe-space around the bottom of the font. Movement of the water is created by a spout that is fed at the plumbing source, away from the font, by hot and cold water faucets. On the opposite side of the spout is a overflow drain, achieved by cutting into the rim of the stone and leading the water into the sewer system. Depending on whether a big sound or just a trickle is desired, the faucet is turned on high or low. The water only flows when people are present. Once a week the water is removed by emptying it through a drain in the bottom. Cleaning consists of wiping calcium deposits off the black granite at water level with a commercial cleaner-solvent. Parishes that shy away from any additional maintenance can be reminded that cleaning a polished surface is not very involving. Surrounding this font, to make any use of water natural and generous, is a circle of slate tiles. *Illustration 74* shows how well this font works for infant baptism.

Illustration 75 shows the clarity of purpose in the bucket-like baptismal tub: Sins will be washed away here. While the parishioners have totally accepted the concept of the baptismal tub, built in 1978 of the same rosewood as the altar, ambo and presider's chair, visitors are usually stunned by the direct and blunt approach to the sacrament of cleansing. Staves of wood, which are narrow strips placed edge to edge to form the sides and the lining of this vessel, have been glued together and are held tightly by a metal loop. It is good to see how earthy these vessels are. Not too long ago, before the use of running water, there were tubs used for regular weekly bathing, and today they are favorites in health spas.

73. Notice that the carpet has been cut away so that water can be splashed.

73

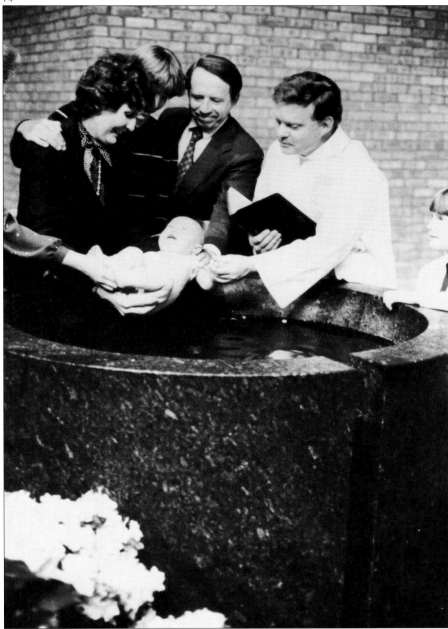

74. A toe space at the bottom of this font allows people to get close to the water.

75. Like any tub, this font has a metal band holding it together and making it beautiful.

77

77. This lead tub shows Christ the teacher.

76. Wooden tubs are shown here as auxiliary fonts for the baptism of an entire family.

78. Elevated on three lion feet, this tub depicts Christ rising out of the waters of baptism. The Latin inscription says: "When this sacrament is administered, the simple element of water causes through the power of the word gifts of salvation. For the new Adam is born and the old one dies."

Metal Tubs

Though wooden tubs have been used since the eleventh century for baptism, none of them have actually survived, except in paintings depicting candidates immersed in a tub full of water *(illustration 76)*. In contrast, there are still a great number of metal tubs that have escaped decay, such as the ornate Romanesque lead tub from England *(illustration 77)*.

The bronze font from 1226 CE in *illustration 78* is elevated on three lion feet. Christ is buried in a mountain of water.

Parishes that insist on using an immersion font but don't have the budget to match their enthusiasm, often feel encouraged to use a galvanized metal tub *(illustrations 79 and 80)*. Some feel the need to hide the metal with a wooden frame or cloth material, but there is really no need to hide the strong symbol of the washing away of sins, as long as the ambience supports the sacramental character: in this case a self-made wooden deck, to keep the tub off the vinyl floor, a precious cloth for the table that holds the holy oils, candles and garments, and a few plants to signify living water. (Plants, however, should never be used to the point that they become an obstacle to seeing or reaching the water, the primary element of baptism.)

Stone Tubs

Illustrations 81–83 show stone tub fonts from the Romanesque period. The font in *illustration 81* is shaped like a cask, a variation of a tub, whereas the font in *illustration 82* almost looks like a well. The tub font in *illustration 84* has an interesting and legendary history. Before being used as a baptismal font, legend has it that the tub was used to collect the blood of the companions of St. Ursula as they were martyred in Cologne. (See the mural on page 70.) Contemporary stone fonts are shown in *illustrations 85–87*.

More Examples

The tub font in *illustration 88* allows affusion or immersion. The artist-pastor has designed a metal tub by stretching rolled bronze sheeting over a wooden frame and then torching it and acid-dipping it until the desired color was obtained. The rosewood divider, which is common to all the liturgical furnishings in this church, is reminiscent of the metal band which rings around most wooden tubs.

In *illustration 89* the band is used for a symbolic purpose. Combining the design of thorns and laurels, this tub font shows martyrs' fronds. It stands in the crypt of the Berlin

79.

79. This galvanized wash tub—a temporary font—works well for immersion.

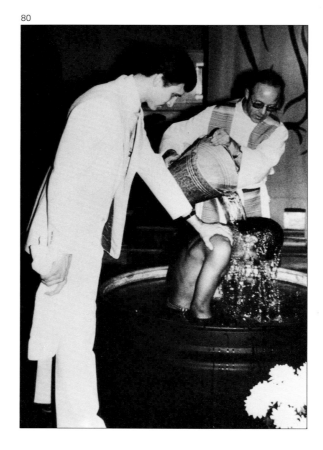

80.

80. While a more elegant container could have been used to pour the water, its abundant use nonetheless speaks of the meaning of baptism as a washing away of sin.

81. The carved lotus flowers symbolize eternal life on this cask-shaped tub.

82. Reminiscent of a well, this font is a good size. Because lids are no longer necessary, the Holy Spirit sculpture could be suspended from the ceiling above the font.

83. This twelfth-century font was renovated in the thirteenth century by the addition of gothic arches chiseled into the sides and by being lifted up onto a pedestal.

84. Legend has it that this tub held the blood of St. Ursula and her companions when they were martyred.

85. Imbedded into the rim of this font are reminders of marine life: sculpted shells, frogs, turtles and crustaceans. A plexiglass lid with two handles is etched with a fishnet design.

87. Some fonts built before the revision of the initiation rites could easily be adapted for immersion. This fine brick font could be built into an immersion pool of the same materials located near the entrance of the church.

86

86. The arena arrangement of two platforms surrounds a circular, centrifugally slanted brick floor. This allows for the pouring of great amounts of water over an adult. The patron saint—St. John Brebeuf—is depicted in the background.

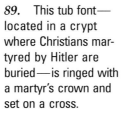

88. This tub is made of bronze sheeting. The rather minimal bowl could be replaced with a deeper one.

89. This tub font—located in a crypt where Christians martyred by Hitler are buried—is ringed with a martyr's crown and set on a cross.

90. This font for a Franciscan church sits at one end of the antiphonally arranged seats, while altar and ambo are at the other.

91. Carved images from St. Francis' canticle celebrate water and the rainbow, the sign of the covenant God made with Noah never to destroy the earth by water again.

cathedral, whose pastor, along with many diocesan priests, was murdered by Hitler. They are either buried or memorialized around the font. A large ceremonial staircase makes the visual connection between the upper and the lower church and proclaims how much the church today depends on the foundation of this heroic sacrament and on the martyrs who took their baptismal vows seriously. The container is made of chiseled sandstone and is lifted off the floor by four strong, simple feet. Matching the bronze wreath is a bronze lid which resembles the simple, unadorned lids of wooden tubs. This is truly a holy place with one gravestone right behind the font and the

wall-mounted Easter candle illuminating both the font and the tomb of those who were "washed clean in the blood of Christ."

Perhaps few churches have such a history to celebrate. But a church can search its past and present to discover some element that identifies it and use this to individualize the font. That was done in the Franciscan church shown in *illustration 90*. The parish chose the canticle of St. Francis to decorate the large tub font. In exquisitely carved detail the praises of water, sun and moon follow the cylindrical shape. The section in *illustration 91* shows how God is making peace in the sign of the covenant after the waters of the flood.

Examples from the East

Finally, *illustrations 92–93* show gleaming copper tubs placed near the iconostasis depicting the angels and patron saints. The Eastern church has never ceased to baptize by immersion. First turning to the west to deny Satan's sinful ways, and then turning to the east to begin the journey towards the rising sun, the candidates determine their orientation (the word means "direction toward the dawn, the east," the victorious Christ). For that they implore the saints depicted in the icons for assistance. But it is in fact the water of the tub that separates one existence from the other.

93

93. Baptismal water containers of the eastern churches are traditionally tub-shaped. Notice the spigots so that the faithful can take holy water home.

92

92. Icons of the holy archangels guard this tub font—and all who are baptized here.

How to Build a Font

In planning a font, a committee can influence how the symbols of baptism in their manifold expressions will speak to the assembly. The building committee has an opportunity that at least the font itself is right, lending itself to a great celebration, no matter what else may go right or wrong. A worthy font, therefore, is essential to guarantee access to baptism and other water rituals that follow in the life of a community. The shape of the font, like the positioning of the altar table and the seating arrangement of the worshipers, is a pivotal point in forming the church in public worship and all the consequences it entails. A well-designed and well-positioned font is proof that a community has understood what it means to be a redeemed people who bring Christ to the world. In short, at the font the validity of a community's ecclesiology is tested.

Preparations

This places a big responsibility on the building committee. At the beginning of the committee's work, the members, as a rule, are not well acquainted with each other, with their work or with the liturgical and scriptural traditions out of which final choices will be made. This changes with each meeting as members learn together about the sacrament and as they share their different experiences of their own church building and the Christian mission that is sacramentally initiated under its roof. As they begin to use the same terms and speak the same language, they become capable of identifying the special character of their own church (both the community and the building) as a prerequisite for choosing a font design.

After the committee identifies the special character of its own church, it is important for it to create a strong scriptural-liturgical basis for understanding the mystery of baptism. Rather than a lecture on the scriptures and its symbols, an opportunity for the parish to encounter them and reflect back on the experience is helpful. The more the church experiences her signs and symbols as a conveyor of the numinous, the more it falls silent or speaks in poetic ways and sings in elevated verses.

One method: Gather the parishioners (don't forget the catechumens) in the church and keep silence around the current font or in the location where the new font is to be built. Well-chosen prayers create the atmosphere:

> Brothers and sisters,
> let us lift up our prayers
> in the same spirit we lift up the cross:
> proclaiming our Lord as
> the way that is no dead end,
> the truth that cannot be silenced,
> and the life that will not be entombed.[1]

Or a hymn might be sung:

> We hold the death of the Lord deep
>   in our hearts.
> Living, now we remain with Jesus
>   the Christ.[2]

A reading from scripture will invite an experience of the Holy One. Romans 6:3–11—the eighth reading from the Easter Vigil—would be a key passage. This reading is so foundational to understanding baptism that the participants may be invited to memorize it. Experience has shown that building committee members and catechumens are not only capable of learning this powerful passage by heart, but they actually enjoy entrusting such thoughts to their memories, to be able to return to them throughout their lives.

Following such a prayer might be a discussion of the images in the reading, the experience of baptism in the parish and in the lives of the individuals present. From this can be discerned the meaning of baptism for this particular community. Using the pictures, drawings and texts in the preceding chapters of this book, the meaning of baptism and its various symbols can be rounded out. The building committee can begin to sense which of the various symbols have the strongest attraction for the parish.

Making Rough Sketches

After the decision has been made about the symbolic shape for the font, sketching will begin. Rough sketches can be made during a meeting of the building committee. It is best to do this on location, so as to immediately discern three things: 1) How the font will function in pointing to the altar, 2) how it will work when the assembly enters the building and people sign themselves, and 3) how the actual participation in baptism can take place.

Rough sketching of several possibilities leads either to a confirmation of the chosen type of design, to its modification, or to its complete abandonment because it would not fill the physical requirements of the sacramental community. These are: to be close to the water, to be able to see the action and hear the words, and to recognize by mere sight that baptism is the sacrament of first order which leads to participation in the eucharistic community around the altar. There should be no hesitation

to change rough sketches frequently until a good solution is found with which everybody is in complete agreement. Sketching does not cost much and is very enjoyable because it is a truly creative moment in the whole process. Changing your mind after design specifications have been drawn up is expensive. A penalty fee may even have to be paid if a change is desired after materials have been cut. However, that sacrifice is at times preferable to not getting the font you had always imagined. Some people find it difficult to visualize what the final result will be when looking at floor plans and elevation drawings only. In that case the building of a simple model will be helpful. Elaborate models, however, are expensive when built by an expert.

Evolving a Design

Illustrations 94–98 show the evolution of a font design achieved through sketching. *Illustrations 94 and 95* are the first rough sketches done by a design artist in the presence of the building committee. They worked with four bodies of water in order to symbolize the four rivers running through Eden. *Illustration 96* shows how the various sketches were then harmonized into a composite. The liturgical consultant then moved the design to the stage shown in *illustration 97*. The four-part font is still shown, but an alternate three-part design is offered as well. (The consultant worried that the four-part font would hinder access to the water and limit the assembly's view.) Finally, the three-part font was chosen and a professional drawing rendered *(illustration 98)*. The resulting font is pictured and discussed on page 55.

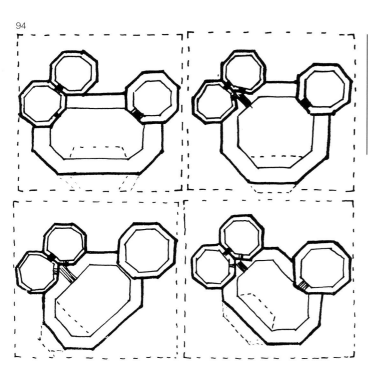

94. The initial design concept was a font of four bodies of water representing the four rivers that run through Eden. Plan views of four initial options.

95

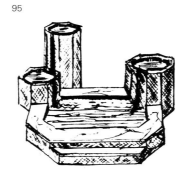

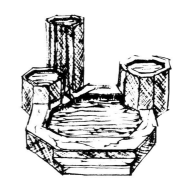

95. Elevation views.

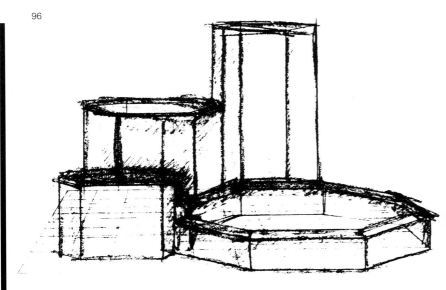

96. The initial sketches were harmonized in this elevation view.

97. The initial design of four bodies of water was then changed to a design using three, close to the final plan.

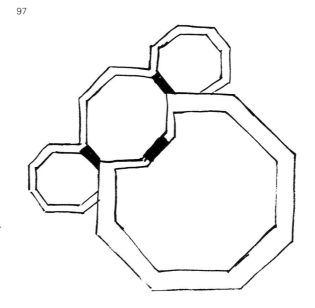

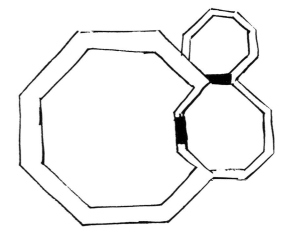

The First Case Study

There are many methods and materials to choose from when building a font. The first case study presented here is the successful building of a six-sided font at Our Lady of the Angels, a Franciscan motherhouse in Wheaton, Illinois. A given in this case were six marble panels of different lengths, taken from the former communion rail. On one side they were decorated with marble inlay, depicting the symbols of six of the sacraments—all but eucharist. These were to face the water. The position of these six marble slabs was marked on the floor *(illustration 99)*. A heavy, fiber-reinforced rubber liner, commercially available by the roll, is the first material that covers the floor. Stainless steel lining or a lead pan are alternatives. The former is expensive, the latter has at times eroded after only a few years, mostly due to the treatment of the seams and the chemical content of the water.

To pay careful attention to this substructural insulation of the font, it is important to know some of the characteristics of water. Water has an enormous weight and exerts it to run toward the lowest possible level. That means that its weight and its desire to escape an embankment apply a constant pressure on the retaining walls of the font. The more water, the greater the pressure. Leakage therefore is the number one challenge to face. If we consider this task seriously as a confrontation between nature and human ingenuity, we might be spared many disappointments and frustrations of a leaking font.

The great weight of the water requires that another preparatory step besides substructural insulation be taken. A structural engineer may

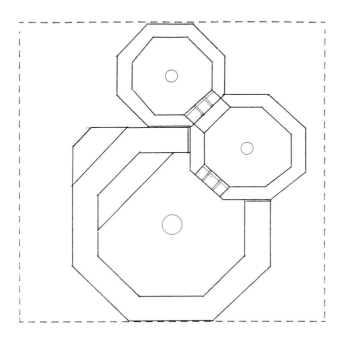

98

ELEVATION   SCALE: 1/2"=1'-0"

98. The final design in elevation and plan views.

be consulted to determine whether the floor is strong enough to carry the weight of the building material in addition to the weight of the water. When in doubt, steel supports can be installed in the area below the floor of the font. If that is not feasible, the structural engineer will suggest other methods of additional support. Most dioceses have the professional service of a structural engineer available.

The Lower Pool. The next step in the building of the hexagonal font was the assembly and erection of the six heavy panels according to the design that had been transferred from the floor to the rubber liner (*illustration 100*). Rubber mallets were used to tap the marble panels into place. A miter-cut of the sides would have been preferable, but with the available panels it would not have resulted in an inner opening of six feet in diameter, which was the goal of the building committee. The panels were held together and attached to the floor by mortar while the inside connection was caulked with water-resistant caulking compound. The compound was applied with greatest care and precision because even the slightest flaw could have resulted in leakage. During each step, it was important to watch that the rubber liner would not be damaged by the enormous weight of the marble or simply by the use of tools or by being stepped on by the workers.

Next, the upright panels were braced by columns of brick, two for each panel. These bricks also served as anchors for the outer wall panels, which were connected by mortar and held together with clamps while the mortar was setting.

100. The panels of the former communion rail are carefully positioned. It is important not to rupture the rubber liner on the floor.

101. A beveled overhang allows a ledge to sit on or rest towels or holy water containers.

101

99. The shape of the font is traced on the floor. Notice the roll of rubber liner about to be laid.

With inner and outer panels in place, patterns were cut, one by one, for the capping stones of each section. They not only form the stabilizing connection between the inner and outer walls but also provide a comfortable rim for seating. A finished look was achieved by installing this seating flush with the outside walls, but permitting a beveled overhang of one inch over the inner walls of the font *(illustration 101)*.

The font was built for a Franciscan church. Its patron saint, St. Francis of Assisi, devoted himself to the mystery of the cross, and he was graced with receiving on his own body the wound marks of the Lord, the stigmata. It was logical then to choose a cross for the inside floor of the hexagonal pool, that, by alluding to Friday, the sixth day of the week, symbolizes Christ's death. The color chosen for the cross inlay was the same red marble used to fashion an upper bowl for the font. Both the upper bowl and the cross inlay match the large marble band that forms the base stone around the interior walls. This choice of stone, then, connected the new font with the rest of the building. The font looks as if it had been built with the structure rather than years later. Often, attention to such detail allows the font to appear indigenous and very appropriate for the building.

The Upper Bowl. The inside bottom of the font has an almost invisible opening, just large enough for a ¾" plastic tube that runs down the short distance to the motor pump, attached to the ceiling immediately below the floor of the font. The upper bowl, also equipped with a floor drain, was crafted in the workshop of the marble cutter. Also a hexagonal-shaped container, it was constructed of seven panels of red marble, one for the bottom and six for the sides *(illustration 102)*. These panels feature the most attractive white vein design. These very veins however, create a problem because they make the marble porous and unsuitable to be used for water, so the marble surface had to be treated with a marine sealer mixed with a hardening compound.

Before the upper bowl was positioned on the rim of the hexagonal pool, two one-inch holes were drilled through the twelve-inch floor to reach the ceiling of the room below. There a small one-unit motor pump that circulates the water was hung. With a dimmer switch, the water flow can be regulated from a trickle to a lively splash. The ceiling to which the motor is attached is covered by a dropped ceiling that hides the motor from view but makes it easily accessible. Placing the motor somewhat away from the actual font area is frequently done to eliminate the unpleasant humming sound of the motor. If desired, a small heating unit and a water filter could be installed near the motor pump. Here it was thought unnecessary.

In this case the font was filled with bottled distilled water to eliminate unwanted chemicals. Replacement due to evaporation is minimal. After the one-time expense, the water is recycled continuously. To keep it clean, one ounce of liquid chlorine was added per 50 gallons of water. A number of chemicals are available commercially to stop algae from growing, calcium deposits from settling at the water

Seven panels of red marble are used to construct the upper bowl, also a hexagon.

line or iron stains from developing. In general, however, people feel hesitant about chemicals and settle for manual maintenance.

In two-tiered fonts such as the one described here, the big moment comes when the motor is turned on and the water begins to circulate. It may be disappointing if the water, instead of splashing out into the lower pool clings to the outer walls of the upper bowl and dribbles down. The "living waters" that the parishioners joyfully anticipated are sadly invisible and/or inaudible. To avoid this, spouts of copper or plastic tubing can be inserted into the wall of the upper basin to reach farther out over the lower pool. Another solution is to place a slab at the rim of the upper container where the overflow occurs. It allows the water to flow away from the upper basin and splash into the lower pool.

In the case of the hexagonal font at Our Lady of the Angels, the opposite problem occurred: The impact of the water created a big splash. Some people loved it, others were disturbed by the noise. A compromise was made by inserting at an angle from the upper basin a plexiglass splashboard about seven inches wide to guide the water from the rim of the upper bowl into the lower pool *(illustration 103)*. This eliminated the noise while leaving the visual impact of the running water that envelops the plexiglass and makes it nearly invisible. Almost every font needs adjustments after it is built, and patience should be practiced until the desired effect is accomplished.

Usually the floor immediately surrounding the font should be of stone—brick, slate, tile, marble or granite—to make it evident that water can be used freely there. Here though, the industrial carpet used in the church was

103. A plexiglass splashboard, barely visible when the font is full and water is flowing, guides the water and lessens the noise of splashing.

extended to the font to avoid an edge that would obstruct a wheelchair. Also, the height of a wheelchair was the determining factor in establishing the height and the position of the upper bowl, so that the water could be reached with ease.

The Font's Surroundings. Creating the font's surroundings is important: A good font can be made ineffective if it is improperly placed in the building. At Our Lady of the Angels, a wrought-iron wreath of light, six feet in diameter and containing 96 light fixtures, was placed over the font. A second wreath was placed over the altar platform *(illustration 104)*. This puts emphasis on the two focal points of sacramental activity: font and table. Each fixture has a dimmer switch and can be lighted separately. A significant Easter candle flanks the font, resting securely in an adequate base *(illustration 105)*.

A strong reason why this baptismal area has become a favored gathering place is the presence of a St. Francis statue, seated on a long

104

104. The font is on the same axis as the altar. The same kind of light fixture that hangs over the altar hangs over the font.

106. (following page) The statue of St. Francis in the shrine beyond the font appears to be resting, contemplating the waters of baptism.

105

105. A significant paschal candle flanks the font.

bench and inviting people to sit down and look at the water *(illustration 106)*. His frail appearance and his air of contemplation invite people to meditate on the water. There are no statues of birds or other animals around the figure of St. Francis. Instead, a single dove was positioned next to the exit where the old holy water font used to be *(illustration 107)*. Masterfully carved of bleached lindenwood, the dove has inserted into its chest a relic of St. Francis and one of St. Clare. Everybody is invited to touch the carving when leaving and renew the prayer of St. Francis, "Make me an instrument of your peace." In this way, font and patron saint and baptismal mission are harmonious. The presence of the holy oils opposite the dove at the entrance further contributes to the unified character of the baptismal place *(illustration 108)*.

A never-ending play of changing colors puts this place into contact with the outside world and the heavens as the modern stained-glass windows throw large patches of color on the water's surface and the surrounding floor. Images in the windows of the great flood and the rainbow of God's covenant lead to the baptismal waters through which Christ makes or renews his personal covenant with each person.

The Second Case Study

When Loyola University of Chicago conducted a major renovation of Madonna della Strada Chapel, the large church that serves the student community, the altar and the ambo were separated and placed on opposite ends (sides) of the space and thereby became two distinct focal points. The assembly was seated on chairs

106

107. A carved dove containing relics of St. Francis and St. Clare sits where a holy water container once hung. People entering the church now bless themselves directly from the font.

108. Near the font, the holy oils are reverently reposed. The candle helps draw attention to them.

in monastic fashion, facing each other during liturgies, as a people fully conscious of and responding to each other as members of the body of Christ.

During the renovation time of almost two years, a building committee set for itself the task of self-education. The members studied church documents, saw slide presentations and debated pertinent questions of sacramental theology, liturgical requirements, pastoral care and catechesis, as well as canon law.

Under the guidance of Jerome Overbeck, a large committee formulated "assumptions" that led to "recommendations." They conveyed the main criteria for the new font to the administration responsible for financing the project as well as to the people who were to conceive and execute the design. The recommendations were so simple and essential that they would be useful almost anywhere:

1. A place for baptism is essential. It is not a luxury item in the regular worship of our community.

2. We prefer that the place for baptism be permanent, considering it more as a place than a piece of furniture.

3. We understand the baptismal font to be a permanent symbol of our entry into the church and into our eucharistic worship.

4. The font should be fully visible to the assembly.

5. Immersion of adults and children needs to be an option because it is the fuller and more appropriate action in baptism.

6. It would be ideal to associate our baptismal water with the water of Lake Michigan, immediately adjacent to the church, to appreciate more fully the natural symbol.

7. We affirm the value of "living water" within our place of worship (more a cascade than a trickle or a spray).

8. Placing the font at the east end, with the three east entrances as the only regular entrances into the church, would make a significant theological statement.

9. We recommend that the design include a pool of water large enough so that water can be poured generously over the whole body of an adult standing or kneeling in the water.

10. The pool could be built on the existing floor of the church.

11. In the design of the pool area the paschal candle will have a prominent position.

12. Attached to the east wall would be a cupboard with a glass door (ambry) to store and make visible the holy oils.

13. We recommend that the baptismal area serve as both the place of entrance and the place for gathering before and after the liturgy.

Making a Model. The artist and the liturgical design consultant spent several silent hours in the church to perceive its architectural elements. The octagonal shape for both upper and lower basin was chosen and affirmed for its symbolic and architectural strength. Assuming that at least two candidates may be baptized simultaneously at any given Easter Vigil, both the artist and the consultant knelt on the floor in the designated area. Bowing deeply, with arms crossed on the chest, they were able to determine how much physical space is needed for the humble gesture of kneeling in the water as a generous amount of water is poured over the entire body. The shape of the lower basin was recorded on paper. The height and width of the upper basin were determined right then in relation to the lower basin and the back wall. A model was built and presented on location to the building committee *(illustration 109)*, which approved shape, size, building material and splashboard. The members also accepted the suggestion to place above the font a symbol that would convey the notion that this place is important. The model was moved to different places in the church, and it became clear that the first choice, at the entrance, under the former choir balcony, was the best location.

Back in his studio the artist built an oak frame that received three coats of polyurethane for protection. Properly treated wood and water have a natural affinity and friendship with each other. Most of the success of this font can be attributed to fine craftsmanship and to the manner in which the upper and lower basin were so simply and harmoniously joined together *(illustration 110)*. A clay model was sculpted for the future bronze splashboard.

Hammering the metal bowl from a large copper sheet was the next step. The upper edge clung to the octagonal shape of the wooden rim and then slowly resolved itself toward the middle into a round shape. This treatment gave the bowl a simple elegance, enhanced even more by the octagonal oak setting.

The opening of the water overflow from the bowl was designed to result in a cascade, not a drip. A plaster cast was taken of the clay model for the splashboard. This mold was sent to a foundry to be cast in bronze *(illustrations 111–112)*.

Inside the housing is a pipe that is connected to the water source by a shutoff valve in the font *(illustration 112)*. While this housing would be a good place for pump, filter and heater, it was decided to suspend this equipment from the basement ceiling directly below the font, lest the humming noise of the motor should be amplified by the wooden structure, much as a cello augments sound. This would distract those who use the chapel throughout the day for moments of peace and quiet.

Any community considering the installation of a new baptismal font must first test the stability of the floor in order to determine whether additional support is needed. At Madonna della Strada none was needed.

An octagonal marble floor was installed in the font. Throughout the renovation, marble was removed from side altars and walls to be recut and reused later. There was sufficient material so that the bottom of the lower container of the font and the inside could be lined, and the wooden substructure of the upper container could be covered. In that way, the most prominent building materials already present in the church—marble, wood and bronze—were combined in the font. The result is that the font looks as if it had always been in its place.

Placement of the Font. A slate tile floor allows the water for baptisms to be poured generously and even spilled. Under new overhead lights, the bronze splashboard channels the water amply and powerfully, glistening with life. The tall paschal candle holder and the open ambry, both carved of oak, pick up patterns present in the church windows. The distinctive setting of the church was enhanced

110

111

110. Fine crafting ensures that the upper and lower portions of this font form a simple, beautiful harmony.

111. A plaster cast was taken of the clay model of the splashboard and sent to a foundry to be cast in bronze.

112

112. The bronze splashboard is functional and beautiful.

114. (following page) The ambry and the paschal candle are on either side of a glass door that frames the font with a view of Lake Michigan.

113

113. Inside the pedestal of the upper bowl is a pipe connected to the water source and a shutoff valve.

by the installation of new plate glass doors in addition to the original bronze doors, so that the waters of Lake Michigan can be seen beyond the font. Chairs can be moved easily into the baptismal area. Suspended above the font are four uneven rings carved of oak, calling attention to the place from all seats of the large church and suggesting the presence of energy or power, the power of the Holy Spirit *(illustration 114)*.

All steps in the renovation of Madonna della Strada chapel and in the construction of this place of baptism were easy and logical. The font looks elegant and spreads the feeling of joy and anticipation among the people. Knowing the architectural elements of a church —its distinctive marks and its weaknesses— may encourage any committee to plan its own font. In preparation, it is necessary to acquire a solidly based baptismal theology, to recognize the particular community's liturgical needs and to impart ideas and concepts clearly to the builder and design consultant. Then, the members of the assembly will someday have a worthy place of baptism in which they are proud to gather.

FOOTNOTES

[1] The prayer is by Linda Murphy in Gabe Huck and Maryann Simcoe, eds, *A Triduum Sourcebook* (Chicago: Liturgy Training Publications, 1983), 40.

[2] David Haas, "Now We Remain" (Chicago: Gregorian Institute of America, 1983).

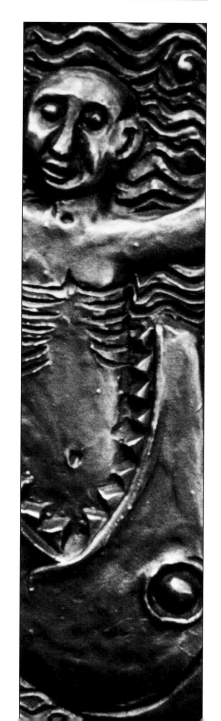

The Location of the Font

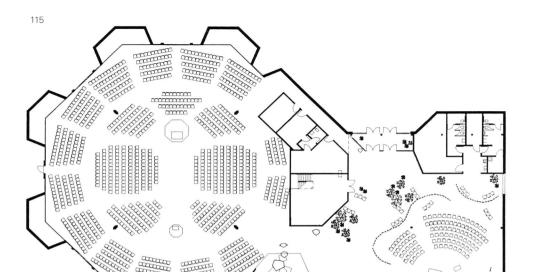

115. The original plan for this church was to locate the font in the narthex but in a separate alcove. The font is actually being built even closer to the main doors, though.

116. Located near the main doors, this font invites all who pass to touch its waters.

117. The main doors make a fitting backdrop for the font, because it is by baptism that we take our places around the Lord's table.

In addition to a font's design, its location in the place for worship reveals something about the meaning of baptism. There are four basic locations, each with its own significance. The font can be located near the entrance or in the narthex, in a separate baptistry, in the midst of the assembly or in the sight line of the altar and ambo. The location of the font will also affect the choice of art to be near it.

Near the Entrance

Locating the font in the narthex near the main entrance of the church signifies that baptism is the sacrament of entry. *Illustration 115* shows a floor plan proposing a font to be built in its own area just inside the main doors. People will pass it as they enter for Mass and will be able to bless themselves with holy water directly from the font. The use of chairs in the main hall allows for seating to be arranged around the font when baptism is celebrated outside of Mass. The font in *illustrations 116 and 117* is also located near the main entrance. The upper level of this font invites all who pass by it to touch its waters. Sprinkling rites begin here.

The font in *illustration 118* is located in a generous space, the narthex. This is a place for people to gather. There is plenty of room for catechumens, sponsors, parents and infants and ministers. There is enough room here to hold the wake of a dead Christian or receive it and sprinkle it with water at the beginning of the funeral Mass. There is enough room here for a bridal party to form a procession or greet guests. There is enough room for groups to gather and pray at other times. The entrance procession forms here.

The relationship between the font and altar is strongly defined by their placement. Here the altar is clearly the destination of the journey that begins at the font, even at the beginning of every Mass.

While the bowl of the font in *illustration 119* is rather small by today's standards, the sunken area in which it stands is instructive. Near the main door of the church, this sunken area is ringed with benches. The benches are seats when baptism is celebrated outside of Mass, but they also keep people from stumbling down the two steps as they enter the room. The fact that the sunken floor is stone suggests that it could be flooded for baptism by immersion. Water from the bronze bowl could be poured over the entire body of the catechumen standing or kneeling in a few inches of water.

A Separate Baptistry

Historically, fonts were located in rooms separated from the main worship hall because catechumens went into the font naked, leaving behind all vestiges of their former lives to

118

118. Notice the generous space around this font. While located in the narthex, the font nonetheless points to the altar.

119. Despite the rather minimal bowl, the sunken area ringed by benches is a fitting place for baptism near the entrance of the church. Perhaps the sunken area—made of stone—could be filled with water for baptizing by immersion.

119

be born again. While the assembly kept prayerful vigil in the main hall, the bishop baptized in the baptistry, assisted by male deacons for the male catechumens and female deacons for the female catechumens. After coming out of the font and being robed, the newly baptized, candles in hand, processed with the bishop back to the assembly, where they were anointed for all to see.

A baptistry then is a chapel for baptism, a place set apart. *Illustration 120* shows how a separate baptistry is a fitting place to house the font. Its ceiling mosaic is of biblical water symbols and a skylight opens the room up to the heavens. The paschal candle is mounted on the wall.

St. Monica Church has a contemporary baptistry with its own seating *(illustration 121)*. This baptistry is located between the gathering space and the main worship hall: To take your place for Mass, you must pass by the font. There is no way into the eucharistic assembly except by way of baptism.

In the Midst of the Assembly

A unique, fitting place to locate the font is in the midst of the assembly. Departing from the notion that the sanctuary is the only holy place in the church building and that all holy actions must go on there, placing the font in the midst of the assembly is a sure sign that the whole place where the church gathers is holy. It is significant when the assembly surrounds the

120. Here is a fitting chapel for the celebration of baptism. The whole assembly cannot fit in here, but it keeps vigil in the adjacent eucharist hall and welcomes the newly baptized into its midst for the chrismation.

font: It is into this people that one is baptized. The local church gives birth to new Christians. A proposal for a renovation in *illustration 122* would have placed the font in the midst of the assembly. The font was later moved closer to the door as the parish became interested in the significance of baptism as entry into the household of faith.

Illustration 123 shows a font located in the midst of the assembly. In celebrations of baptism at this font, the assembly is no passive observer. The closeness of the font invites the assembly to be the primary minister of the sacrament. Here, Mother Church gives birth to her children.

Font, Altar and Ambo

Parishes often choose to locate the font in the sight line of the altar and ambo so that the assembly can see the baptisms at the Vigil or when baptism is celebrated at Sunday Mass. The danger in this decision is that, if not carefully located in a distinct place, a font in the sight line of altar and ambo may give the impression that all sacred actions occur "up there on stage" and that the assembly is a passive observer.

The plan in *illustration 124* shows one way to avoid such a problem. Located in the sight line of altar and ambo, the font is on a separate platform. Placed on a different level, the font has its own area clearly defined.

It is important that water, word and meal each has its own distinct place within the assembly. The renovation of the church in *illustration 125* shows how the former sanctuary apse was turned into the place for baptism. It was a logical choice. When the altar

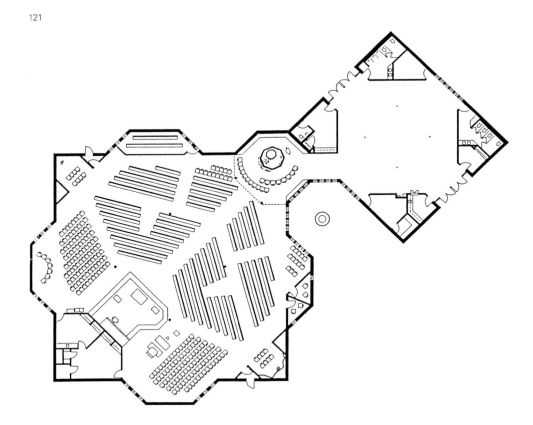

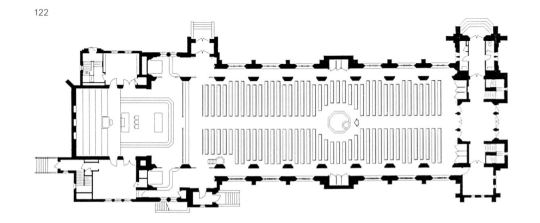

123

124

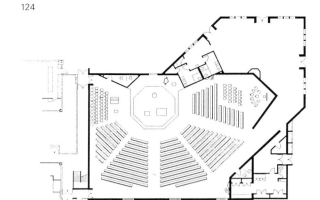

124. In the sight line of altar and ambo, the font is placed on its own platform to avoid the impression that the sanctuary is a stage.

123. Located within the assembly, the font is truly the center of parish life. Turning pews in toward the font gives the font its own distinct place.

125

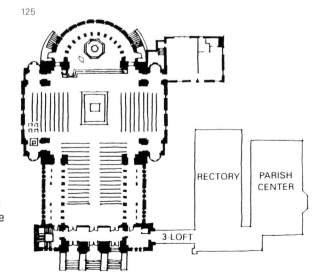

121. This contemporary baptistry is placed between the narthex and the main worship hall. To take your seat for eucharist, you must pass by the font.

122. This renovation proposal puts the font in the midst of the assembly, the church who gives birth in baptism.

125. Here the font is placed in the apse, the former sanctuary. See illustration 126.

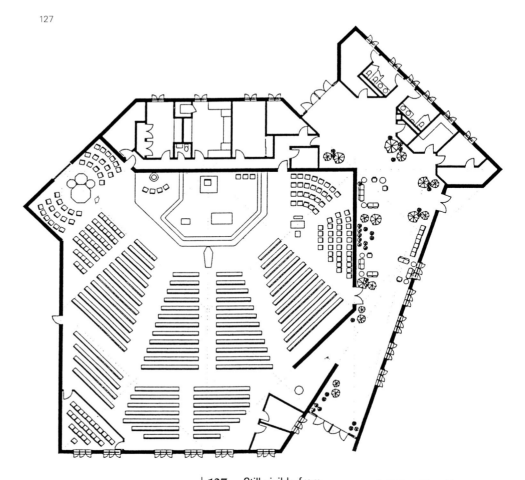

was brought out into the assembly and set on its own island platform, the former sanctuary was empty. The ceiling of the apse has a beautiful painting of the crucifix as the tree of life. Space near the doors was extremely limited. The original ambo was not moved, so a good spatial relationship is established between ambo, font and altar. Each has its own distinct place, and all three places are of different height allowing for maximum visibility. *Illustration 126* shows that the apse with its semicircular colonnade is a splendid setting for the font.

The placement of the font in *illustration 127* shows that it is possible to locate the font in the sight line of the altar and ambo and yet put it in its own alcove. This plan works well when baptism is celebrated at the Vigil or during Sunday Mass: All can see from their seats. When baptism is celebrated outside of Mass, chairs can be rearranged in the alcove to make a proper place for a smaller assembly.

126. The former sanctuary makes a fitting place for the font now that the altar is in the midst of the assembly.

127. Still visible from the assembly's seats, this font is in its own alcove. Baptism can be easily celebrated within or apart from Mass.

128. Plumbing—a practical matter—can be both functional and beautiful.

129. The Book of Life stands near the font, holding the names of those baptized and buried from this place.

Art for the Font

Wherever the font is located, the place for baptism will help to reveal the mystery of Christian initiation when works of art accompany a beautiful font. The place needs to be functional and sincere, but that does not mean barren or impoverished. The outdoor fountain in *illustration 128* shows how plumbing—a practical matter for immersion fonts—can be functional and beautiful at the same time. The well-designed spigot is pleasing in form; its ornamentation reflects the carving in the stone. The Book of Life in *illustration 129* is also functional and beautiful. Placed near the font, the book holds the names of all who are baptized in or buried from the font during the years. The book is a good size, the stand is low and sturdy and the candles are in good scale. These are objects worthy of being near the font.

Baptistry Doors

When the font is located near the main entrance of the church or in its own baptistry, the nearby doors are significant. In addition to being functional passageways, they are symbols of baptism as entry into the church. The door to the baptistry in *illustration 130* is literally the door to paradise. In the lower left corner are Adam and Eve in the Garden of Eden about to sin. In the upper right corner, Christ hangs on the cross, redeeming all sinners, tended by Mary. These images are the last things seen before encountering the font.

The bronze knocker on the baptistry door in *illustration 131* shows Jonah rising to new life after spending three days in the belly of the whale. This image is often used in baptistries. A bronze panel from another baptistry in *illustration 132* makes the connection between Jonah and baptism even more explicit. Jonah's stance is that of one raised to new life, and the waters resemble the waters of baptism.

The Floor around the Font

The font is a place for using water abundantly. This requires that the floor surrounding the font can withstand splashing and spilling water. Varieties of stone and tile are hence the best materials to use, and they can be as beautiful as they are practical. Surrounding the font with floor mosaics is an ancient custom (see the fonts on pages 20 and 40). A contemporary example is found in *illustration 133*.

130

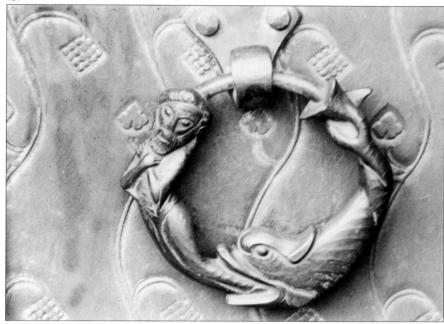

132. This bronze panel from a baptistry makes the connection between Jonah and baptism explicit. The waters resemble the waters of baptism, the whale resembles a font, and Jonah stands as one raised to new life.

131. A knocker on a baptistry door shows Jonah rising out of the belly of the whale. This is a favorite image in older European baptistries.

130. These baptistry doors are literally the doors to paradise—lost by Adam and Eve but regained by Christ, who dies attended by Mary.

133

133. A contemporary floor mosaic. Varieties of stone and tile are good to use near the font, as they can withstand getting wet.

134. A mat woven of vegetable fibers looks as rich as a wool rug but is not damaged by water.

135. This tapestry gives dignity to the place for baptism.

136. The detail shows that baptism into the death of Christ promises the blossoming of new life.

135

The font in *illustration 134* is surrounded by a mat woven of plant fiber. While it has the appearance of a rich wool carpet, it is not damaged by water. It is safe to stand on, and it frames the font with dignity.

Walls and Windows

The dignity and importance of the font can be emphasized by works of symbolic art placed on nearby walls. The tapestry in *illustration 135* was created to hang behind the font. The detail shown *(illustration 136)* shows how baptism into the death of Christ promises the blossoming of new life.

136

The fish is an ancient symbol worthy to be near the baptismal font. Besides the obvious connection to water, the fish is one of the first symbols Christians used for Christ. The Greek word for fish, *ichthys*, was interpreted as an acronym for the Greek words meaning "Jesus Christ, God's Son, Savior," a brief and early version of a creed. The wrought iron sculpture in *illustration 137* adorns a baptistry wall in Cologne.

An early Greek word for the sacrament of baptism meant "enlightenment," so the connection between baptism and light suggests that stained-glass windows near the font are appropriate. The windows behind the font in *illustration 138* depict biblical passages important to baptism. They are, from left to right: (top row) Jonah and the whale; the baptism of Jesus; Jesus raising the dead (evoking Romans 6); (bottom row) the exodus through the Red Sea; the baptism of the Ethiopian by Philip (Acts 8); the elect receiving the robe washed white in the blood of the Lamb (Revelation 7).

More abstract, the window in *illustration 139* shows how baptism, represented by the waves, leads to eucharist, represented by the loaf and fish. This window is situated between font and table.

The celestial symbolism in the window in *illustration 140* reminds those who stand at the font before it that all times and seasons belong to Christ. By virtue of baptism, Christ is our light, the center of our universe.

Canopies

A canopy or sculpture over a font points to its importance and draws attention to it in a large

137. This wrought iron fish hanging on a baptistry wall recalls an ancient creed: "Jesus Christ, God's Son, Savior."

138. The windows behind this font depict biblical passages important to baptism.

139. An early Greek word for baptism meant "enlightenment." The use of windows in the place of baptism is appropriate.

140. The celestial symbols of this window suggest that baptism leads to heaven.

away in the Red Sea, a jug of water-turned-to-wine at Cana in Galilee, the Holy Spirit descending in the form of a dove. The canopy defines the place for baptism, making it visible from all points in the church.

The use of canopies or sculptures overhead is not a new idea. The sixteenth-century font in *illustration 144* is flanked by two marble columns holding up a beautiful, ornamental stone brace from which an iron cross is hung. The symbol speaks clearly.

141. The carved wooden rings suggest the Holy Spirit hovering over the waters of the font.

142. A ring of light over the font defines it as a holy place. A similar one over the altar makes the connection between baptism and eucharist.

143. This canopy helps define the place for baptism in a large room. Etched into the glass are symbols evoking biblical water stories.

space. The carved-wood sculpture in *illustration 141* suggests the Holy Spirit hovering over the waters. Beyond the font and through the door are seen the waters of Lake Michigan. Notice the location of the ambry with oils and the paschal candle.

A ring of light over the font in *illustration 142* helps define it as a sacred place. An identical ring over the altar at the other end of the axis speaks of the connection between font and table. In one place life is given; in the other life is sustained.

The steel canopy and etched glass over the font in *illustration 143* depicts familiar biblical water symbols: Noah's ark, Jonah and the whale, the rock that yielded water when struck by Moses in the desert, chariot wheels swept

The location of the font and the art that accompanies it must never obscure the font and the primary symbol it holds, water. The mystery of baptism is well served by beautiful art, however. The importance of baptism in the life of the church suggests that the place for baptism be adorned with loving care.

144. Canopies over fonts are not new, as this elegant sixteenth-century example testifies.

144

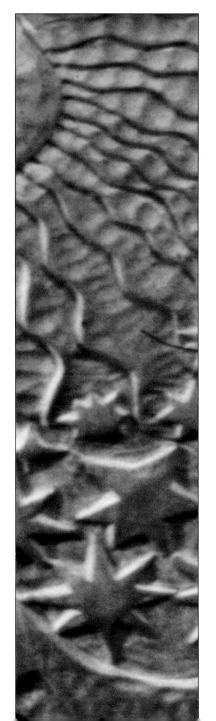

Temporary Vessels

145. Salad bowls are poor substitutes, but this beautiful Steuben glass bowl has its own granite stand.

146. This commercially produced stone bowl is an alternative to the parish punch bowl.

A place for baptism is so crucial to the life of the parish that no one should rest easy until a place is renovated fittingly or a new place is built. That takes time, though, and in the interim, baptisms will still be celebrated. Here are some temporary solutions. But given the fact that temporary often becomes permanent, they are offered cautiously. It should be clear from reading the preceding chapters that a temporary font by nature is inadequate to serve the mystery of baptism.

Bowls

Since the baptistry is a separate room, Easter water for Sundays is kept in a large Steuben glass bowl near the ambo in *illustration 145.* Salad bowls placed on the altar are poor substitutes for fonts. But this beautiful bowl has its own sturdy stand and is near the ambo.

To avoid the punch bowl look, investigate the use of commercial stone containers to hold water from the font. The stone bowl in *illustration 146* is 20 inches in diameter.

A beautiful clay bowl can serve as a fitting water container. The handmade bowl in *illustration 147* has a 30-inch diameter and sits on a low table ornamented with clay tiles.

The commercially produced bowl in *illustration 148* was loaned by a garden supply store owner for use as a temporary font. Its

147. A handmade clay bowl serves as an appropriate temporary water vessel.

148. If necessary, sometimes suitable alternatives can be found at garden supply stores.

149. This beautiful tub has eight carved panels showing biblical water scenes.

151. While rather small, this temporary font is beautifully designed and built of field stones and cement.

150

150. A large clay pipe was transformed into a temporary font by a parish artist who decorated it with tiles.

simple design and wide opening allow for a good quantity of water to be seen.

The problem with all these temporary vessels however, is that they hold a minimum of water.

Deeper Containers

When deeper temporary vessels are used, they tend to hide the water. The beautiful tub in *illustration 149* has eight carved panels showing biblical water scenes. Its lining is hammered copper.

The large clay pipe in *illustration 150* was transformed into a temporary vessel for baptismal water by a parish artist who decorated it with a tile mosaic.

152. This detail shows the beauty of a temporary drinking well hastily constructed by Roman soldiers with stones at hand.

153. When forced to use a temporary font, a parish need not sacrifice some degree of beauty.

Temporary and Beautiful

The temporary vessel in *illustration 151* was built of field stones and cement. While it is small and rather minimal, it is beautifully designed and executed. The candle stand is of proper size. The framed stained-glass window from a demolished church shows the victorious Lamb of God. It serves as a fitting standard to accompany this temporary font.

Wherever they traveled along the Rhine, Roman soldiers built small wells from stones at hand *(illustrations 152 and 153)*. The simple beauty of these hastily constructed wells shows that if forced to use a temporary font, a parish need not sacrifice some degree of beauty. Skills in the community can be mobilized to their full extent. Nothing, however, can ever really substitute for a permanent place for baptism— the most beautiful font, carefully located and lovingly adorned, that the parish can achieve.

EPILOGUE

The title of this book, *A Place for Baptism,* reveals a tension between two concepts which are opposites. Yet taken together they succinctly express the essence of Christian faith and life: the tension between the finite and the infinite. A place, a circumscribed space, denotes finitude. Baptism, "the washing of water with the word that brings about the life of eternity" (Tertullian), denotes infinitude, a mystery accessible only in faith. How can the rich mystery of baptism be located in a place? In the preceding pages, both the details of place and the many meanings of baptism have been explored. A necessary and fitting conclusion is a brief reflection on what the localization of the holy at the celebration of baptism implies for the subsequent daily life of the newly baptized—and of the church— in a secular world.

The original meaning of the Latin word *sacramentum* is bonding. A sacrament is that through which one is bound to someone else. It denotes an oath of allegiance or, in Judeo-Christian terminology, a covenant. A full understanding of that basic meaning accomplishes two things. First, it does away with the all-too-common notion that Christian initiation is a process that ends with graduation at the font. Second, it raises the existential question of the consequences of a covenant that sends forth the newly baptized from the place for baptism into their daily environment as a new creation, irrevocably bound to the suffering, death and resurrection of Christ.

The various rites leading up to baptism, confirmation and eucharist convincingly address these consequences, the privileges and obligations of being a member of the mystical body of Christ. They include a rite which, given the turmoil and complexities of contemporary culture, may seem at worst obsolete, at best antiquated or irrelevant: exorcism.

The Roman rite offers several options for exorcism before baptism; the language of all the options is unambiguous and powerful. It asks God to protect the catechumens "from the spirit of evil," to save them from "the tyranny of the enemy," and, in the celebration of baptism, it elicits from the catechumens themselves the resolution to "reject Satan, the father of sin and prince of darkness" and "all his works and all his empty promises." With these words the sacramental rite initiates the newly baptized into a battle that, in the worldview not only of Christianity but of all monotheistic religions, has raged from the beginning of creation. It will not end until Christ has "made everything new." Taken seriously and understood in all of its demanding implications, it is a cosmic battle, one that challenges the catechumens to rise above a "living room/bedroom faith" and join a battle that is both intensely personal and truly "catholic"— all-embracing.

Admittedly, contemporary culture permits no easy access to such a cosmic vision of the Christian faith. It is a vision that arose from a Christian faith still unencumbered by those "sicknesses unto death" that characterize Western modernity: skepticism, atheism, moral and ethical relativism and nihilism. Yet there is ample evidence that contemporary Christianity is returning to what used to be a unanimous Christian conviction until the Enlightenment: The fullness of the message of salvation cannot be grasped unless the life of Jesus is seen as a mortal combat between him and Satan. A reading of the gospels shows that Satan is omnipresent in the life of the Lord. Satan is to Jesus the ruler of this world and the source of darkness, the tempter who tries to seduce Jesus into accepting what the world celebrates as power and achievement, the one who tries to dissuade Jesus from accepting his passion and the one who puts betrayal into the heart of Judas. Satan sifts the disciples like wheat, takes the seed of the word from the mouth of those who receive it. When the hour of his passion comes, Jesus recognizes it as the hour of Satan, "the hour of the power of darkness."

It is out of this vision of Christian faith as a struggle against cosmic evil that many of the fonts of past ages, and some contemporary ones, incorporate a symbol of Satan, such as the serpent, into their design. These artistic representations reinforce and make permanently visual what the words of the exorcism say. They are a constant reminder that those who have been baptized into the suffering, death and resurrection of Jesus have now joined the Lord in his continuing mortal battle against the one whom he called a murderer from the beginning, the father of lies, and the prince of darkness. When seen with the eyes of Jesus, the evil of our age, whether manifest in unemployment, drug addiction, violence in the streets, world-wide famine, epidemics or war, loses the mask of being an abstract "issue" and is seen for what it truly is: the work of Satan. The extent and profundity of evil and horror in today's world escape any logical, analytical or scientific explanation.

Personified radical evil, whether called the devil, Satan, Lucifer, or the Evil One, is a mystery, but more so is the incarnation of the living God. In the finite place for baptism the church struggles against evil by immersing catechumens and infants in the infinite goodness of God. Thus at the place for baptism the baptized leave behind at the font an anemic, emaciated and ultimately sterile view of the world and enter into the inexhaustible richness and grandeur of an all-embracing vision of life—life for God in Christ.

ILLUSTRATION CREDITS

Unless otherwise indicated, photographs are by Regina Kuehn.

1. Photo: Jerome Riordan.

2. A four-lobed pool in a house atrium, Mexico. Photo: Richard Grimmel.

3–4. Mural, "Healing of the Man Born Blind," circa 1072–87 CE, Sant' Anselmo in Formis.

5. Catholic cathedral, Trier, Germany.

6. St. Maria im Kapitol, Cologne, Germany.

7. St. John the Baptist Church, Pelham Manor, New York. Executed by Diprato-Rigali, Park Ridge, Illinois.

8. St. John the Baptist Church, New Ulm, Germany. Dominikus Boehm, architect.

9. All Saints Church, Basel, Switzerland.

10–11. St. Marcelline Church, Schaumburg, Illinois. Donald Walpole, OSB, liturgical design consultant.

12. St. Ambrose Cathedral, Des Moines, Iowa. Robert Rambusch, liturgical design consultant. Photo given to the author by the cathedral.

13. St. Peter baptizing, mural in the village church (built 1129 CE), Idensen, Germany.

14–15. St. Francis Church, Concord, California. Frank Mighetto, architect. Photos: S. Anita Stauffer.

16. St. Francis Church, Concord, California. Frank Mighetto, architect. Photo: Frank Mighetto.

17–18. Crypt baptistry, Cathedral of Speyer, Germany.

19. Sketch of an ancient cruciform font: Hart McNichols, SJ.

20. Memorial of Moses, Mount Nebo, Jordan. Photo: Maria Leonard.

21. Bronze sculpture by Egino Weinert, Cologne, Germany.

22. Enamel, Cologne, Germany. Egino Weinert, artist.

23. "Christ's Descent into Hell," painting at the Wallraf-Richartz Museum, Cologne, Germany.

24. Roman sarcophagus, late third century CE, Roman-Germanic Museum, Cologne, Germany.

25. St. Procopious Abbey Church, Lisle, Illinois. Edward Dart, architect.

26. Mosaic at the mausoleum of the cardinals of the Archdiocese of Chicago, Hillside, Illinois.

27. St. Martin Church, Chicago, Illinois. Regina Kuehn, liturgical design consultant.

28. Tradition holds that this is the well where Jesus met the Samaritan woman, Nablus, Israel. Photo: Jerome Riordan.

29. A pre-Christian pool with iron grill cover, Cologne, Germany.

30. St. Martin Church, Chicago, Illinois.

31. Our Lady of Hope Church, Mount Prospect, Illinois. David Hasselhofer, designer-architect.

32–33. St. Margaret Mary Church, Naperville, Illinois. Paul Straka, architect.

34. Byzantine icon of the baptism of Christ, fourteenth-century, Greek Patriarchate of Jerusalem.

35. Mural of the baptism of Christ, circa 1250–70 CE, at the cathedral, Parma, Italy.

36. Icon of Christ baptizing in the Jordan River, Kondakof Institute, Moscow, Russia.

37. Memorial of Moses, Mount Nebo, Jordan. Photo: Maria Leonard.

38. Ruin of St. John the Baptist Church, Ephesus, Turkey. Photo: Eric Lies, OSB.

39–41. First Baptist Church, Oak Park, Illinois.

42. Bethel Bible Church, Chicago, Illinois.

43. From a sales catalog selling immersion tanks for Baptist churches.

44–48. St. Benedict the African Church, east worship site, Chicago, Illinois. Belli and Belli, architects and engineers. Regina Kuehn, liturgical design consultant.

49. St. Benedict the African Church, east worship site. Photo: Belli and Belli.

50. Magnus Haus, Cologne, Germany.

51. Divine Providence Church, Westchester, Illinois. John C. Voosen, architect. Regina Kuehn, liturgical design consultant.

52–55. St. Luke Church, River Forest, Illinois. John C. Voosen, architect of the renovation and new font. Marchita Mauck, liturgical design consultant.

56. Cathedral of Ss. Peter and Paul, Indianapolis, Indiana. E. A. Sovik, design architect. Photo: Catholic Communications Center, Archdiocese of Indianapolis.

57. St. Elizabeth Seton Church, Orland Hills, Illinois. Belli and Belli, architects. Joseph Aspell, SM, designer and builder of font.

58–60. St. Monica Church, Chicago, Illinois. John C. Voosen, architect. Regina Kuehn, liturgical design consultant. Robert Harmon, stained-glass artist.

61–62. St. Clement Church, Chicago, Illinois. Walker Johnson, architect for the new font. Diprato-Rigali, builders. Photos: Maria Leonard.

63. St. Clement Church, Chicago, Illinois. Photo: Bob Sprengel.

64. Holy Angels Church, Chicago, Illinois. Todd Halamka, architect. Regina Kuehn, liturgical design consultant.

65. Our Lady of the Angels Church, Wheaton, Illinois. Don Galassini, builder. Regina Kuehn, liturgical design consultant.

66. Tapestry detail, Metropolitan Museum of Art, New York, New York.

67. Oil painting showing the baptism of St. Ursula, 1450 CE, Wallraf-Richartz Museum, Cologne, Germany.

68. Oil painting showing the baptism of the companions of St. Ursula, 1450 CE, Wallraf-Richartz Museum, Cologne, Germany.

69. Medieval font, Marquette University, Milwaukee, Wisconsin.

70. Our Lady Help of Christians Church, Chicago, Illinois. Regina Kuehn, liturgical design consultant.

71. Commercial containers on the plaza of the Emperor William Memorial Church, Berlin, Germany.

72. St. Michael Church, Hirzbrunnen, Switzerland. Photo: Mark Scott.

73–74. St. John of the Cross Church, Westchester, Illinois. Edward Dart and Paul Straka, architects.

75. St. John Neumann Church, St. Charles, Illinois. Robert Rambusch, liturgical design consultant.

76. Tapestry, 1402 CE, from the Tournay Cathedral, France.

77. St. James Church, Gloucestershire, England. Font circa 1130–1140 CE.

78. From the cathedral at Osnabrueck, Germany, 1226 CE.

79–80. St. Francis de Paolo Church, Chicago, Illinois.

81. Great St. Martin Church, Cologne, Germany.

82. Circa 1056–1075 CE, St. Georg Church, Cologne, Germany.

83. St. Kunibert Church, Cologne, Germany.

84. St. Andreas Church, Cologne, Germany.

85. St. Englebert Church, Germany. Hildegard Domizlaff, artist.

86. St. John Brebeuf Church, Niles, Illinois. John C. Voosen, architect.

87. Church of the Atonement, Holweide, Germany. Rasch and Wolsky, architects.

88. Our Lady of the Mount, Cicero, Illinois. Richard Grimmel, font designer.

89. Martyrs' font, St. Hedwig Cathedral, Berlin, Germany.

90–91. St. Clare College Church, Clinton, Iowa. Jerzy Kenar, sculptor. Regina Kuehn, liturgical design consultant.

92. An eastern rite church, Santa Fe, New Mexico.

93. Ss. Vladimir and Olga, Chicago, Illinois.

94–98. Divine Providence Church, Westchester, Illinois. Laverne Holden, font designer.

99–108. Our Lady of the Angels Church, Wheaton, Illinois. Don Galassini, builder (font). Jerzy Kenar, sculptor (St. Francis statue, dove reliquary). Regina Kuehn, liturgical design consultant.

109–114. Madonna della Strada Church, Loyola University, Chicago, Illinois. Jerzy Kenar, sculptor. Jerome Overbeck, SJ, renovation coordinator. Regina Kuehn, liturgical design consultant.

115. Plan for St. Bernard Church, Lockport, Illinois. John C. Voosen, architect.

116–117. Church of the Holy Spirit, Schaumburg, Illinois. Ben Nelson, architect. Steve Melahn, leaded-glass artist. John Buscemi, liturgical design consultant.

118. St. John the Evangelist Church, Hopkins, Minnesota. George Rafferty, architect. Frank Kacmarik, liturgical design consultant. William Woeger, FSC, project coordinator. Photo from *Worship Space*, a slide collection sponsored by the Federation of Diocesan Liturgical Commissions, 1983.

119. Cathedral at Trier, Germany. Photo: Mark Scott.

120. Cathedral at Wuerzburg, Germany. Bronze font, 1279 CE. Ceiling mosaic by K. Clober, 1967.

121. Plan for St. Monica Church, Chicago, Illinois. John C. Voosen, architect. Regina Kuehn, liturgical design consultant.

122. First plan for renovation of St. Luke Church, River Forest, Illinois. John C. Voosen, architect. Marchita Mauck, liturgical design consultant.

123. Our Lady Help of Christians Church, Chicago, Illinois. Regina Kuehn, liturgical design consultant.

124. Plan for Our Lady Mother of the Church, Chicago, Illinois. John C. Voosen, architect.

125. Plan for renovation of St. Clement Church, Chicago, Illinois. Walker Johnson, architect for the renovation. Bill Beard, drawing.

126. St. Clement Church, Chicago, Illinois. Photo: Bob Sprengel.

127. Plan for Divine Providence Church, Westchester, Illinois. John C. Voosen, architect. Regina Kuehn, liturgical design consultant.

128. Fountain in the marketplace, Munich, Germany.

129. St. Alban Church, Cologne, Germany.

130. Paradise Door, St. Alban Church, Cologne, Germany. Toni Zenz, design and execution.

131. Bronze knocker, St. Alban Church, Cologne, Germany.

132. Bronze panel for baptistry, Cologne, Germany. Egino Weinert, artist.

133. St. Willibald Church, Munich, Germany. Floor mosaic by Franz Mayer Studio of New Jersey.

134. Church at Burnham Norton, Norfolk, England.

135–136. Tapestry, designed and executed by Robert Harmon. Our Lady Mother of the Church, Chicago, Illinois.

137. Wrought iron wall sculpture, St. Alban Church, Cologne, Germany.

138. St. Eberhard Church, Stuttgart, Germany.

139. Window, Our Lady Mother of the Church, Chicago, Illinois. Robert Harmon, artist.

140. Window, designed and executed by Giotto Moots, OP, Sagrado Art Studios, Santa Fe, New Mexico.

141. Madonna della Strada, Loyola University, Chicago, Illinois. Jerzy Kenar, sculptor.

142. Our Lady of the Angels, Wheaton, Illinois.

143. St. Hugo of the Hills, Bloomfield Hills, Michigan. Robert Rambusch, liturgical design consultant. Photo: Charles Tines.

144. Ruins of a sixteenth century font and canopy, Istria, Yugoslavia.

145. Stueben glass, St. John Abbey, Collegeville, Minnesota.

146. Commercial stone container, St. Catherine/ St. Lucy Church, Oak Park, Illinois.

147. Clay water vessel. Veronica Fremont, potter.

148. Temporary font set up in the 1970s at Holy Name Cathedral, Chicago, Illinois.

149. Carved portable font. Jerzy Kenar, sculptor.

150. Temporary font, Holy Name of Mary Church, Chicago, Illinois.

151. St. Meinrad Archabbey Church, St. Meinrad, Indiana.

152–153. Roman-Germanic Museum, Cologne, Germany.